CAMBRIDGE
UNIVERSITY PRESS

CAMBRIDGE ENGLISH
Language Assessment
Part of the University of Cambridge

Cambridge English

CAMBRIDGE OFFICIAL PREPARATION MATERIAL

FIRST for Schools 1

FIRST CERTIFICATE IN ENGLISH FOR SCHOOLS

WITH ANSWERS

AUTHENTIC EXAMINATION PAPERS
FROM CAMBRIDGE ENGLISH
LANGUAGE ASSESSMENT

For revised exam from 2015

Cambridge University Press
www.cambridge.org/elt

Cambridge English Language Assessment
www.cambridgeenglish.org

Information on this title: www.cambridge.org/9781107647039

First published 2014

Printed in the United Kingdom by Latimer Trend

A catalogue record for this book is available from the British Library

ISBN 978-1-107-64703-9 Student's Book with answers
ISBN 978-1-107-69267-1 Student's Book without answers
ISBN 978-1-107-66907-9 Audio CDs (2)
ISBN 978-1-107-67209-3 Student's Book Pack (Student's Book with answers and Audio CDs (2))

Contents

Introduction

This collection of four complete practice tests comprises papers from the *Cambridge English: First for Schools* examination; students can practise these tests on their own or with the help of a teacher.

The *Cambridge English: First for Schools* examination is part of a suite of general English examinations produced by Cambridge English Language Assessment. This suite consists of five examinations that have similar characteristics but are designed for different levels of English language ability. Within the five levels, *Cambridge English: First for Schools* is at Level B2 in the Council of Europe's *Common European Framework of Reference for Languages: Learning, teaching, assessment*. It has been accredited by Ofqual, the statutory regulatory authority in England, at Level 1 in the National Qualifications Framework. *The Cambridge English: First for Schools* examination is widely recognised in commerce and industry and in individual university faculties and other educational institutions.

Examination	Council of Europe Framework Level	UK National Qualifications Framework Level
Cambridge English: Proficiency *Certificate of Proficiency in English (CPE)*	C2	3
Cambridge English: Advanced *Certificate in Advanced English (CAE)*	C1	2
Cambridge English: First for Schools *First Certificate in English (FCE) for Schools*	B2	1
Cambridge English: Preliminary *Preliminary English Test (PET)*	B1	Entry 3
Cambridge English: Key *Key English Test (KET)*	A2	Entry 2

Cambridge English: First for Schools follows the same format as *Cambridge English: First* and the level of the question papers is identical. The only difference is that the content and treatment of topics in *Cambridge English: First for Schools* have been particularly targeted at the interest and experience of school pupils. *Cambridge English: First for Schools* candidates who achieve Grade C or higher in the exam, receive a *Cambridge English: First for Schools* certificate.

Further information

The information contained in this practice book is designed to be an overview of the exam. For a full description of all of the above exams, including information about task types, testing focus and preparation, please see the relevant handbooks which can be obtained from Cambridge English Language Assessment at the address below or from the website at: www.cambridgeenglish.org

Cambridge English Language Assessment
1 Hills Road
Cambridge CB1 2EU
United Kingdom

Telephone: +44 1223 553997
Fax: +44 1223 553621
Email: helpdesk@cambridgeenglish.org

The structure of *Cambridge English: First for Schools*: an overview

The *Cambridge English: First for Schools* examination consists of four papers.

Reading and Use of English 1 hour 15 minutes
This paper consists of **seven parts**, with 52 questions. For Parts 1 to 4, the test contains texts with accompanying grammar and vocabulary tasks, and separate items with a grammar and vocabulary focus. For Parts 5 to 7, the test contains a range of texts and accompanying reading comprehension tasks.

Writing 1 hour 20 minutes
This paper consists of **two parts** which carry equal marks. In Part 1, which is **compulsory**, candidates have to write an essay of between 140 and 190 words, giving their opinion in response to a task. In Part 2, there are four tasks from which candidates **choose one** to write about. The range of tasks from which questions may be drawn includes an article, an email/ letter, an essay, a review and a short story. The last question is based on a set text. In this part, candidates have to write between 140 and 190 words.

Listening 40 minutes (approximately)
This paper consists of **four parts**. Each part contains a recorded text or texts and some questions, including multiple-choice, sentence completion and multiple-matching. Each text is heard twice. There is a total of **30 questions**.

Speaking 14 minutes
The Speaking test consists of **four parts**. The standard test format is two candidates and two examiners. One examiner takes part in the conversation while the other examiner listens. Both examiners give marks. Candidates will be given photographs and other visual and written materials to look at and talk about. Sometimes candidates will talk with the other candidate, sometimes with the examiner, and sometimes with both.

Grading

The overall grade is based on the total score gained in all four papers. All candidates receive a Statement of Results which includes a profile of their performance in each of the four skills and Use of English. Certificates are given to candidates who pass the examination with grade A, B or C. Candidates who achieve grade A receive the *Cambridge English: First for Schools* certificate stating that they demonstrated ability at Level C1. Candidates who achieve grade B or C receive the *Cambridge English: First for Schools* certificate stating that they demonstrated ability at Level B2. Candidates whose performance is below B2 level, but falls within Level B1, receive a Cambridge English certificate stating that they have demonstrated ability at Level B1. Candidates whose performance falls below Level B1 do not receive a certificate.

For further information on grading and results, go to the website (see page 5).

Test 1

READING AND USE OF ENGLISH (1 hour 15 minutes)

Part 1

For questions **1–8**, read the text below and decide which answer (**A**, **B**, **C** or **D**) best fits each gap. There is an example at the beginning (0).

Mark your answers **on the separate answer sheet.**

Example:

0 **A** effects **B** tricks **C** skills **D** talents

0	A	B	C	D
	▭	▬	▭	▭

BMX racing

Somewhere in California during the early 1970s, a bunch of kids customised their bicycles so they could do **(0)** .... on them. They were able to do incredibly **(1)** .... things like jumping off ramps and making their bikes fly through the air. Then they began racing them along dirt tracks. The kids were recorded on camera and the **(2)** .... film, which was called *On Any Sunday*, **(3)** .... the word about the new pastime like wildfire. And so a sport **(4)** .... by kids for kids was born. Bicycle Motocross was the name given to it, which was soon shortened to BMX. It **(5)** .... the attention of thousands of kids over one short summer.

Nowadays, BMX racing is recognised as a fun action sport. BMX caters for the individual. Every rider gets to take **(6)** .... No one sits on the bench and no one ever gets **(7)** .... from the team. And statistics have proved that, due to the **(8)** .... safety requirements, it is one of the safest of all youth sports. Have you ever thought of giving BMX a try?

1	**A**	exceptional	**B**	impossible	**C**	excellent	**D**	impressive
2	**A**	resulting	**B**	following	**C**	concluding	**D**	developing
3	**A**	broadened	**B**	extended	**C**	spread	**D**	passed
4	**A**	composed	**B**	created	**C**	formed	**D**	set
5	**A**	took	**B**	earned	**C**	paid	**D**	caught
6	**A**	place	**B**	part	**C**	position	**D**	play
7	**A**	sent	**B**	left	**C**	dropped	**D**	thrown
8	**A**	harsh	**B**	strict	**C**	firm	**D**	strong

Part 2

For questions **9–16**, read the text below and think of the word which best fits each gap. Use only **one** word in each gap. There is an example at the beginning (**0**).

Write your answers **IN CAPITAL LETTERS on the separate answer sheet.**

Example: | **0** | I | S |

Dolphins on the phone

Did you know it **(0)** .... not just humans who talk? Dolphins do too. And in Hawaii, a female dolphin and her baby have even **(9)** .... a conversation over the telephone! The call was made in an aquarium where the two dolphins swam in separate tanks connected by a special underwater audio link. **(10)** .... they were in different tanks, the two dolphins began whistling and chirping to each **(11)** .... immediately – typical dolphin chatter.

'Information seemed to be passed back **(12)** .... forth very quickly,' explains Don White, a researcher at the aquarium where the experiment took place.

But **(13)** .... exactly were the dolphins saying? **(14)** .... is the question scientists are trying to answer by studying both wild and captive dolphins in the hope that they might **(15)** .... day understand their secret language. They haven't completely cracked the code yet, but they are listening and learning! So who knows? Your next phone call could **(16)** .... from a dolphin!

Part 3

For questions **17–24**, read the text below. Use the word given in capitals at the end of some of the lines to form a word that fits in the gap **in the same line**. There is an example at the beginning (**0**).

Write your answers **IN CAPITAL LETTERS on the separate answer sheet.**

Example: | **0** | S U G G E S T I O N S |

Can plants talk?

Have you ever done any gardening? If so, do you have any **(0)**	**SUGGEST**
on how to speed up and encourage the **(17)** .... of plants?	**GROW**
Surprisingly, some gardeners recommend talking or playing music	
to them, and now a group of British **(18)** .... have found that this	**SCIENCE**
(19) .... may not be quite as crazy as it seems. They discovered	**BEHAVE**
that some young plants make a clicking sound in their roots which is so	
quiet that humans are unable to hear it. The researchers used special	
(20) .... to capture these noises; then when they played the	**EQUIP**
(21) .... back to other young plants, they made an amazing	**RECORD**
(22) .... – the plants actually grew towards the noise. This seems	**DISCOVER**
to suggest that plants can communicate with each other in a way that	
experts were previously **(23)** .... of.	**AWARE**
It could be that sounds and vibrations are used by plants to share	
(24) .... information about growing conditions or about possible	**VALUE**
dangers from pests. Perhaps more people should try talking to	
their plants!	

Part 4

For questions **25–30**, complete the second sentence so that it has a similar meaning to the first sentence, using the word given. **Do not change the word given.** You must use between **two** and **five** words, including the word given. Here is an example (**0**).

Example:

0 Prizes are given out when the school year finishes.

PLACE

Prize-giving .... end of each school year.

The gap can be filled by the words 'takes place at the', so you write:

Example:	0	*TAKES PLACE AT THE*

Write **only** the missing words **IN CAPITAL LETTERS on the separate answer sheet.**

---

25 The bike is quite old so you should ask someone to check the brakes before you ride it.

GET

This bike is quite old so you should .... before you ride it.

26 I borrowed my sister's car because I hadn't yet saved enough money to buy my own.

UNTIL

My sister .... I had saved enough money to buy my own.

27 I was late for school because I couldn't find my bag.

TIME

I .... for school if I'd been able to find my bag.

28 Nicky is the only person who has signed up for the trip.

NOBODY

Apart .... their name down for the trip.

29 I regret not listening to my teacher today.

WISH

I .... attention to my teacher today.

30 'I'm very sorry but we haven't got any more chocolate ice cream,' said the waiter.

RUN

'I'm very sorry but we .... chocolate ice cream,' said the waiter.

Part 5

You are going to read an extract from a novel about an American teenager called Bonnie. For questions **31–36**, choose the answer (**A**, **B**, **C** or **D**) which you think fits best according to the text.

Mark your answers **on the separate answer sheet.**

Queen Rider

Bonnie Wyndham got out of her mother's car and looked at Almonside School. 'I'll make you sorry I've come here,' she told her, pleasantly. Her mother was getting out of the other door at the time so she didn't hear, but Bonnie wouldn't have cared if she had. Her mother knew her feelings. Mrs. Wyndham looked about her. Almonside was a funny school, all bits and pieces, buildings hidden away amongst the trees on a wooded hillside; very confusing at first sight. Then she saw the signs on a post: science block, gymnasium, riding centre ...

'Riding centre,' said Bonnie, showing a sudden interest.

'Headmaster's study,' said her mother. 'This way.'

Bonnie followed her mother along a broad drive that curved between trees.

'I wish you'd walk beside me instead of following me like a dog,' said Mrs. Wyndham wearily, but she didn't seem to expect Bonnie to do so.

A few minutes later, her mother was talking to Bonnie's new headmaster in his study, while Bonnie herself sat and waited outside the door. Suddenly, Bonnie jumped up. 'Why should I just sit here?' she said to herself. 'I'll be thrown out before very long, anyway,' she said mentally to the door, 'so why not get it over and done with?' She left the building and headed for the riding centre in the direction indicated by the sign.

There was a nice old building where the horses were kept, and a large structure for indoor riding. Bonnie looked about her, but there was no one in sight. There was a certain reverence about her manner as she approached the animals. Bonnie treated horses with respect. The horses were very well looked after, she could tell that at once.

Almost every stall was occupied, and she wandered along looking carefully at each horse and judging it. 'They know what they're doing here,' she told a small pony as she ran a finger along its nose. It was the next horse that pulled her up short. 'But aren't you the best of the lot!' she said. He was brown with a touch of white. Lively, probably, but Bonnie liked that. 'You know, I have the feeling we've met before,' said Bonnie, stroking his neck. 'It was in my dreams and I was riding you to victory in some big competition.' Over the stall was his name: Maverick.

Suddenly, she couldn't resist the temptation to ride the horse. 'I wonder where I can find a bridle for your head, and a saddle for your back. Can't be far away.' The room containing all the riding equipment was – Bonnie was delighted to discover – unlocked. Absorbed in the pleasurable task of putting a saddle on Maverick's back, she forgot all about her mother and the headmaster. When she sat up high on the big horse outside the building, she felt like a queen, mistress of all she could see. Her nickname at her previous school had been Queen Bee, and she laughed delightedly as she remembered it. 'You're the best horse I've ever sat on, Maverick,' she said admiringly, 'and when I say that I'm not kidding, I can assure you, because I know about horses, even if I don't know about anything else.'

She nudged him into a walk, then into a trot. 'If I stay here, I think you and I could be great friends,' she confided. She went round and round the paddock. The rhythm was exhilarating, a little breeze whipping smartly past her cheek and making it glow. She could tell Maverick trusted her, and she felt certain that he'd jump well.

31 What do we learn about Bonnie's mother in the first paragraph?

- **A** She was used to being obeyed by Bonnie.
- **B** She had a favourable first impression of the school.
- **C** She had difficulty finding her way around new places.
- **D** She was aware of Bonnie's attitude to her new school.

32 Why did Bonnie leave her seat outside the headmaster's office?

- **A** She was eager to go riding as soon as possible.
- **B** She was unwilling to spend any time on her own.
- **C** She didn't think it would make any difference if she behaved badly.
- **D** She didn't think her mother would take her to see the horses.

33 How did Bonnie feel when she was looking at the horses?

- **A** excited to recognise a horse she already knew
- **B** impressed by the high standards at the riding centre
- **C** anxious to make sure that the horses would like her
- **D** nervous about being seen with the horses

34 What does 'pulled her up short' mean in line 41?

- **A** made her stop in surprise
- **B** made her a bit frightened
- **C** made her feel sorry
- **D** made her change her mind

35 When Bonnie was sitting on Maverick's back she felt

- **A** confident of her riding abilities.
- **B** determined to prove what she could do.
- **C** amused that she had tricked her mother.
- **D** relieved that she had left the past behind.

36 What do we learn about Bonnie by the end of the text?

- **A** She is looking forward to taking up an exciting hobby.
- **B** She is concerned about making new friends.
- **C** She is beginning to feel more positive about the school.
- **D** She is disappointed about having so little time with the horses.

Part 6

You are going to read an article about two teenagers who send a small model man into space. Six sentences have been removed from the article. Choose from the sentences **A–G** the one which fits each gap (**37–42**). There is one extra sentence which you do not need to use.

Mark your answers **on the separate answer sheet.**

Model man in space

At the young age of 17, Mathew Ho and Asad Muhammad have already sent a man into space – a very small model of a man, that is.

Mathew and Asad attached a four-centimetre-tall model man and four cameras to a balloon and launched the whole thing into space. **37** The boys could hardly believe their success, especially as the entire project had cost them just $400. They had worked on it every weekend for four months. It wasn't a school project; they just thought it would be a cool thing to do. 'We didn't really think it would work until that point,' says Mathew.

Mathew and Asad had the idea for the project two years ago when they saw an online video of a balloon being sent into space by some university students. **38** They both had a passion for all things flight-related so they were the perfect partners for the project.

The pair were soon spending every Saturday at Mathew's house, drawing up plans and building the balloon. 'People would walk in, see us building this weird thing with a parachute, and wonder what we were doing. We'd just say, 'We're sending cameras into space!' Mathew had already made a lightweight box to carry the cameras. **39** They needed ones which could be programmed to take photos every 20 seconds without stopping.

Next they sewed the parachute, which took them three weeks on Asad's mum's sewing machine. 'We soon realised that we're no experts at sewing,' laughs Mathew. 'We broke ... what, four needles? Ridiculous!' The end result didn't look too great but worked perfectly. **40** 'People were yelling at us,' remembers Asad.

They ordered a professional weather balloon online, and bought helium gas from a party supply store. Mathew purchased a special wide-angle video camera. Finally, they put the whole thing together, carefully cutting a space inside the lightweight container for three cameras and a mobile phone with a GPS system which helped them to follow it. **41** They also checked with the relevant authorities to make sure its flight wouldn't interfere with air traffic or be illegal.

The boys chose a local football field as their take-off point. Then they blew up the balloon, let it go, and watched their model man float upwards. **42** Less than two hours later, a signal on Mathew's computer told them that the model man had re-entered the earth's atmosphere. He had just landed in a field, 122 kilometres from the launch point. Based on their calculations, the balloon had climbed to about 24,000 metres in just over an hour. Then it exploded, triggering the model man's 32-minute fall to earth. Mathew and Asad have since received a note of congratulations from the manufacturers of the little model man.

A It was just the sort of thing they thought they might be able to do themselves.

B Therefore they needed to calculate where the model would land, based on the take-off point, the weather and the size of the balloon.

C At seven kilometres, they lost both the mobile phone and GPS signals so they went home and made dinner.

D They watched as it landed 97 minutes later, having recorded an astonishing video clip from 24 kilometres above sea level.

E So, with a budget of $500 in mind, they started looking for some which were reasonably priced.

F As a finishing touch, they stuck their model astronaut onto the outside of the box, and found him a tiny national flag to hold.

G They tested it by dropping it off the roof of the building where Mathew lives, which annoyed some of the residents.

Part 7

You are going to read an article in which four teenagers talk about part-time work. For questions **43–52**, choose from the teenagers (**A–D**). The teenagers may be chosen more than once.

Mark your answers **on the separate answer sheet.**

Which teenager

argues that having a job encourages people to be more efficient?	**43**	
says there is only a limited range of jobs to choose from?	**44**	
has to put up with people teasing them?	**45**	
hopes to find regular part-time work eventually?	**46**	
puts up with a general disadvantage of having a job?	**47**	
can choose to work less when short of time?	**48**	
got a job to please someone else?	**49**	
doesn't agree with the reason behind someone's decision?	**50**	
was not told off for a mistake they made?	**51**	
did what they could to improve their situation?	**52**	

Saturday jobs

A Keith

I work in a department store on Saturdays, selling men's clothes. My friends mostly work as waiters at the weekend, or deliver newspapers in the mornings before school. They make fun of me because I spend all my time folding shirts. (I'm not particularly fond of doing it.) But I earn a good hourly wage and work in a pleasant environment so I don't care what they say. When I'm older it'll pay for my driving lessons – then I won't need any more lifts to work from Mum. And it's quite flexible – basically, I can give it a miss when I have too much homework. I even have a staff discount card which makes me very popular with my parents! And at the end of each shift, I'm able to buy reduced-price food in the food hall – a big advantage as I'm always hungry!

B James

I wasn't too bothered about getting a Saturday job, but my father talked me into it – he'd done that sort of thing when he was a kid, and he felt he'd learned a great deal that way. So I started looking. I soon found myself spending Saturdays in a local chemist's. The hours were long, and the pay was rubbish, but then I persuaded my friend Tom to join me so it wasn't too bad. It also helped me to get my next job – I now work in a little supermarket round the corner. I think my dad was right – I've become far more independent, and I've learned a lot about people. Some of the customers come in and chat for hours! Like the other people I work with, I have less time to party because I have to get my schoolwork done as well. But when I do go out, I have a bit of money to spend – so it's worth it.

C Caroline

I've never had a part-time job before, but I recently started babysitting for family friends from time to time. It seems to be the most common job among my classmates as it's not badly paid and the kids are nice. One of my friends helps at children's parties, but there doesn't seem to be that much around for teenagers, apart from babysitting. The only other job I've had was as a waitress at a friend's mother's birthday party. I'm pleased to say I only had one incident involving a bowl of soup which I tipped down the side of a sofa, but the people were very reasonable about it. At some point I'd like a better-paid Saturday job, partly to subsidise my ever-increasing collection of clothes, but also for the experience, as I think I could learn a lot from it.

D Freya

I was going to start a Saturday job at a hairdresser's, but Mum changed her mind about it at the last minute, saying I was wrong to risk letting my schoolwork suffer. Working part-time might leave me with less time for schoolwork I suppose, but she overestimates how much time I actually spend on it. Most people I know do something, even if it isn't every week, mainly babysitting for their parents' friends. I think if you work a few hours every week you learn to organise your time better. Now I tend to spend ages on the Internet and chatting to friends. I'm sure I wouldn't do that if I was working – I'd be too busy! But my mum has made her mind up so there's nothing I can do about it.

WRITING (1 hour 20 minutes)

Part 1

You **must** answer this question. Write your answer in **140–190** words in an appropriate style.

---

1 In your English class you have been talking about the best way to spend your free time. Now your English teacher has asked you to write an essay for homework.

Write your essay using **all** the notes and giving reasons for your point of view.

What is the best way for you to spend your free time?

Notes

Write about:

1. who you spend your free time with
2. what you do
3. .... (your own idea)

Part 2

Write an answer to **one** of the questions **2–5** in this part. Write your answer in **140–190** words in an appropriate style **on the separate answer sheet**. Put the question number in the box at the top of the answer sheet.

---

2 You see this announcement in an international magazine for teenagers.

> **Articles wanted**
>
> **An Interesting Festival**
>
> We are looking for articles about interesting festivals in different countries. Describe one festival in your country and explain what people do. Say why you think it is an interesting festival.
>
> The best articles will appear online next week.

Write your **article**.

3 This is part of a letter you have received from your English friend, Tom.

> As you know, I've been studying science and languages at school for several years now. Next year I have to choose one or the other for my main course of study. Which do you think I should choose and why?
>
> Write soon,
>
> Tom

Write your **letter**.

4 You have seen this announcement in a new English-language magazine for schools.

> **Stories wanted**
>
> We are looking for stories for our new English-language magazine for teenagers. Your story must begin with this sentence:
>
> *Lara saw something unusual on the grass and she went to take a closer look.*
>
> Your story must include:
>
> - a discovery
> - a journey

Write your **story**.

5 Answer the following question based on the title below.

Macbeth by William Shakespeare

Your English class has had a discussion about the characters in the story of *Macbeth*. Now your teacher has asked you to write an essay for homework answering these questions:

- How does the behaviour of Macbeth change during the story?
- Why does this happen?

Write your **essay**.

LISTENING (approximately 40 minutes)

Part 1

You will hear people talking in eight different situations. For questions **1–8**, choose the best answer (**A**, **B** or **C**).

---

1 You hear part of a news item about a school project.
What have the students at the school invented?

A an unusual means of transport

B a method of making ice cream

C a way of producing energy

2 You hear a teacher talking to her students about a writing competition.
What is she doing?

A encouraging them to go in for it

B suggesting how they could do well in it

C correcting information they've received about it

3 You hear part of a radio item about a bird.
The presenter is explaining why

A the bird has the appearance it has.

B the bird has arrived at a wildlife centre.

C the bird was given the name Manukura.

4 You hear two friends talking about a TV talent show.
What do they agree about?

A The girl band made a surprising choice of song.

B The singer who ended the show had a very strong voice.

C The performers were generally better than in previous weeks.

5 You hear a girl talking about a sports event she took part in.
What is the girl doing?

A giving her opinion about people at the event

B explaining why she did so well in the event

C describing what happened at the event

6 You hear a teacher telling her class about something called World Oceans Day.
What is the teacher going to do next?

A give more information about the importance of oceans

B listen to suggestions about how to celebrate the day

C say how the class could help the environment

7 You hear an announcement about a festival.
What is the speaker's main purpose?

A to describe the event

B to publicise a competition

C to explain how to get tickets

8 You hear a boy leaving a voicemail message for his friend.
Why is he calling his friend?

A to offer to do something

B to complain about something

C to give advice about something

Part 2

You will hear a boy called Joe giving a class presentation about a project he's done on the subject of gorillas. For questions **9–18**, complete the sentences with a word or short phrase.

Gorillas

The thing that first got Joe interested in gorillas was a [**9**] he saw as a child.

Joe's uncle saw gorillas in the south of Uganda whilst working as a [**10**] there.

The species Joe's uncle saw in Uganda were [**11**] gorillas.

Joe used a website called [**12**] .com as the main source of information for his project.

Joe uses the word [**13**] to describe the way that gorillas usually behave.

Joe discovered that, as well as vegetation, [**14**] sometimes form part of the gorilla's diet.

The name [**15**] is used to refer to the young males in a group.

Joe says that gorillas choose the [**16**] as the place to build their nests.

Joe explains that [**17**] are the main threat to gorillas.

Joe recommends a book entitled *Gorillas in the* [**18**] for finding out more about them.

Part 3

You will hear five short extracts in which teenagers are talking about a recent holiday. For questions **19–23**, choose from the list (**A–H**) the opinion each speaker expresses. Use the letters only once. There are three extra letters which you do not need to use.

A The best bit was meeting someone who's become a close friend.

B I was good at an activity I hadn't tried before.

C I had a great time performing in a musical event.

D A new experience was more enjoyable than I'd expected.

E The journey to our destination was my favourite part.

F I was proud that I could speak the local language.

G It was more exciting than previous visits to the same place.

H It was good to go away with people for the first time.

Speaker 1		**19**
Speaker 2		**20**
Speaker 3		**21**
Speaker 4		**22**
Speaker 5		**23**

Part 4

You will hear an interview with a writer called Clare Watson, who writes novels for teenagers. For questions **24–30**, choose the best answer (**A**, **B** or **C**).

---

24 What first made Clare want to become a novelist?

A the encouragement of a teacher

B her own passion for reading

C positive feedback from her brother

25 Clare says that her favourite novel

A turned out as she hoped it would.

B is more amusing than her others.

C is the first in a series.

26 Where does Clare get the ideas for her stories?

A They often have their origins in her dreams.

B They come to her when she's exercising.

C They appear when she least expects them.

27 How does Clare feel about the TV series that features one of her characters?

A She wishes it had been made years ago.

B She's glad that other people write the scripts.

C She thinks the actors have been well chosen.

28 What inspired Clare to set up writing groups?

A a conversation with other authors

B letters she received from readers

C a similar project she heard about

29 How did Clare feel when she won an award?

A honoured because her favourite writer had won it before

B apprehensive about how it might change her life

C surprised because she didn't feel she was the best

30 Clare says she can write well about how teenagers feel because

A she's got very clear memories of herself at that age.

B she's in regular contact with teenage relatives.

C she spent several years of her life as a teacher.

SPEAKING (14 minutes)

You take the Speaking test with another candidate (possibly two candidates), referred to here as your partner. There are two examiners. One will speak to you and your partner and the other will be listening. Both examiners will award marks.

Part 1 (2 minutes)

The examiner asks you and your partner questions about yourselves. You may be asked about things like 'your home town', 'your interests', 'your career plans', etc.

Part 2 (a one-minute 'long turn' for each candidate, plus a 20-second response from the second candidate)

The examiner gives you two photographs and asks you to talk about them for one minute. The examiner then asks your partner a question about your photographs and your partner responds briefly.

Then the examiner gives your partner two different photographs. Your partner talks about these photographs for one minute. This time the examiner asks you a question about your partner's photographs and you respond briefly.

Part 3 (4 minutes)

The examiner asks you and your partner to talk together. You may be asked to solve a problem or try to come to a decision about something. For example, you might be asked to decide the best way to use some rooms in a language school. The examiner gives you some text to help you but does not join in the conversation.

Part 4 (4 minutes)

The examiner asks some further questions, which leads to a more general discussion of what you have talked about in Part 3. You may comment on your partner's answers if you wish.

Test 2

READING AND USE OF ENGLISH (1 hour 15 minutes)

Part 1

For questions **1–8**, read the text below and decide which answer (**A**, **B**, **C** or **D**) best fits each gap. There is an example at the beginning (**0**).

Mark your answers **on the separate answer sheet**.

Example:

0 **A** managed **B** arrived **C** succeeded **D** reached

0	A	B	C	D
	▬	▭	▭	▭

Captain of a team

What are the secrets of success in sport? After winning a big match, players are often asked how they **(0)** .... to do it. Most say it is the result of hard work and practice. But another important **(1)** .... in their success is their team captain. The players **(2)** .... on the captain to motivate them and **(3)** .... they all play well together as a team. The role of captain only **(4)** .... a person who works well under pressure. Could you be a captain? Can you take **(5)** .... of a group of people, even when they are tired or frustrated? Can you ensure that the team achieves its full **(6)** .... during a match? It's not easy, but those who do this well are rewarded with a team of players who respect them and **(7)** .... them. **(8)** .... they may not win every match, they will do everything they can to make the captain proud of them. That's the secret of success.

1	**A**	feature	**B**	factor	**C**	mark	**D**	characteristic
2	**A**	rely	**B**	trust	**C**	believe	**D**	hope
3	**A**	prepare	**B**	provide	**C**	enable	**D**	ensure
4	**A**	fits	**B**	suits	**C**	matches	**D**	applies
5	**A**	direction	**B**	order	**C**	responsibility	**D**	charge
6	**A**	talent	**B**	ability	**C**	potential	**D**	promise
7	**A**	catch up with	**B**	look up to	**C**	come up with	**D**	get up to
8	**A**	However	**B**	Despite	**C**	Although	**D**	Even

Part 2

For questions **9–16**, read the text below and think of the word which best fits each gap. Use only **one** word in each gap. There is an example at the beginning (**0**).

Write your answers **IN CAPITAL LETTERS on the separate answer sheet.**

Example: | 0 | M | O | R | E |

Horses

Surprisingly, there are **(0)** .... than 350 different breeds of horse around the world. Many of them can live for up **(9)** .... 30 years. A male horse is called a gelding or a stallion, and a female horse is **(10)** .... as a mare. The height of a horse is measured in 'hands', a hand being the distance **(11)** .... a man's wrist to the tip of his middle finger. The tallest horse ever recorded was Sampson, who lived in the 1850s and stood at over 21 hands.

Horses use facial expressions to communicate emotions. If you know **(12)** .... to look for, their nostrils, eyes and ears will help you to interpret their feelings. Their eyes are positioned on the sides of their head, enabling them to see behind them and making **(13)** .... easier for them to detect predators. They also have the ability to turn **(14)** .... ears from side to side, **(15)** .... is particularly important for wild horses because they need to know where danger is **(16)** .... from.

Part 3

For questions **17–24**, read the text below. Use the word given in capitals at the end of some of the lines to form a word that fits in the gap **in the same line**. There is an example at the beginning (**0**).

Write your answers **IN CAPITAL LETTERS on the separate answer sheet.**

Example: | 0 | O B V I O U S L Y |

Fun with science

So you think science is boring? Well, you have **(0)** .... never been on	**OBVIOUS**
one of our Mad Science courses! We run classes which are designed to	
wake up your imagination and also develop your **(17)** .... of how the	**UNDERSTAND**
world around you works. Working in teams, or **(18)** .... if you prefer,	**INDIVIDUAL**
you get the chance to try a whole range of experiments and then build	
your own robot to take home at the end of the day. Each group of young	
scientists has a set of **(19)** .... to work from, and tutors are there to	**INSTRUCT**
help if anything is at all **(20)**	**CLEAR**
The activities are so **(21)** .... that you will forget that they are also	**ENJOY**
(22) .... ! Our courses run all day, from 10 am to 5 pm and are held	**EDUCATION**
at several different **(23)** .... around the country. The courses are very	**LOCATE**
popular and **(24)** .... is limited so make sure you book early!	**AVAILABLE**

Part 4

For questions **25–30**, complete the second sentence so that it has a similar meaning to the first sentence, using the word given. **Do not change the word given**. You must use between **two** and **five** words, including the word given. Here is an example (0).

Example:

0 Prizes are given out when the school year finishes.

PLACE

Prize-giving .... end of each school year.

The gap can be filled by the words 'takes place at the', so you write:

Example:	**0**	*TAKES PLACE AT THE*

Write **only** the missing words **IN CAPITAL LETTERS on the separate answer sheet**.

---

25 I'd like to be an actor one day but fame doesn't interest me.

INTERESTED

I'd like to be an actor one day but I'm .... famous.

26 I didn't go skating because I was too tired.

WOULD

I .... I hadn't been so tired.

27 It's been absolutely ages since I last saw David.

SEEN

I .... absolutely ages.

28 Can you tell me the difference between these two computers?

DIFFERENT

Can you tell me how .... from that one?

29 It was windy and raining but we still went to the beach.

SPITE

We went to the beach .... and rain.

30 Dad had bought everything we needed before I arrived at the supermarket.

GOT

By the .... supermarket, Dad had bought everything we needed.

Part 5

You are going to read an extract from a novel about a Canadian teenager called Rex. For questions **31–36**, choose the answer (**A**, **B**, **C** or **D**) which you think fits best according to the text.

Mark your answers **on the separate answer sheet.**

Kayak Rex

I leapt from my bed, lifted a corner of the bedroom curtain, and looked down on the river bend. A fresh crack in the ice glistened in the morning sunlight. I shaded my eyes and looked upstream towards the wall of sandbags, there to protect the buildings from flooding as the river ice melted. My back still ached from lifting them into place. All last week, I'd worked alongside most of the town's adult population for long hours, proving I was up to the task. Not that my grandfather took much notice.

With one hand still on the curtain, I swept my eyes along the half-mile ribbon of steaming black water formed by the release pipe from the wood processing factory in Milltown. With fragile ice shelves on either side, the dark open patch was followed by solid ice downstream. As I took off my pyjamas and reached for my kayaking wetsuit, I spotted a boy on the far side of the river's edge – a boy I didn't recognise. I frowned. Unbelievably, he was attempting to balance on an ice shelf along the water warmed by the factory. I zipped up my wetsuit and reached for my kayaking jacket. I checked the pocket for the lucky chain I keep there – a silver chain my famous grandfather once brought back from an expedition in South America. Far better than having a famous grandfather is having this chain, which no one but him, my mom and me know about. Plus, I have the actual diary that he kept on that journey. I keep it under my pillow and read bits of it before I fall asleep. I patted the chain again and made my way towards the kitchen.

'Morning, Rex.' Mom smiled at me as I grabbed a banana off the kitchen counter. 'You're up early for a Saturday. I'll cook up brunch after your training session. Be careful now.' 'Thanks, Mom.' I headed down the hallway, nearly slamming into Grandpa's tall thin frame as he stepped out of his bedroom. 'Can't you ever watch where you're going?' he shouted. 'Where are you going, anyway?' 'Sorry, Grandpa. I'm going kayaking.' As if my wetsuit didn't make that obvious. As if he didn't see me in my kayak every morning. Grandpa is Grandpa, and I try to ignore it when he loses his temper, but he's been making it that much harder for me to do lately.

'What's the point of training? You didn't win the competition,' he said. For a split second, the steel-edged remark hit exactly like he meant it to. But I took a deep breath and silently counted to three. He crossed the hall and slammed the bathroom door shut behind him. Mom appeared with a sympathetic smile. 'Don't mind him. He's ...' '... not himself at the moment,' I finished for her. I refrained from saying that he'd always been that way. But, like Mom, I try to go easy on him.

When I was a child, he was my hero – from the time he first showed me photos of him in the *National Geographic* magazine. Those faded photos still hang framed on his bedroom wall, above his dust-covered expedition medals and trophies. But I don't go into his room anymore. I've got my own growing collection of trophies to look at and, someday soon, maybe, my own face in *National Geographic*. And yet, well, a part of me still wants to remain devoted to him, this ill-tempered old man.

Mom smiled. 'At least, he's coming out of his bedroom more. Have a good session, Rex. I admire your determination to keep it up, even on these cold days!' I smiled back at her as I peeled my banana. 'It'll be warmer in South America,' I said. 'If I come up with sponsors for my expedition.' She laughed and returned to the kitchen. I ate my banana and went downstairs. Stepping into the backyard, I hurried towards the boathouse.

31 How did Rex feel as he looked at the sandbags?

A satisfied with the work he had done
B eager to get down to the river
C relieved that the flooding was over
D concerned he might have to move them again

32 When Rex 'frowned' in line 19, it showed that

A he wished he were outside with the boy.
B he was trying to remember the boy's name.
C he disapproved of the boy's actions.
D he was unable to make out what the boy was doing.

33 What do we learn about Rex's grandfather in the third paragraph?

A He has little idea of what is going on.
B He is behaving increasingly badly.
C He needs more and more attention.
D He is often in the way.

34 How did Rex react to his grandfather's comment about the competition?

A He decided that his grandfather hadn't intended to hurt him.
B He wanted to reply to his grandfather but wasn't sure what to say.
C He hoped to annoy his grandfather by pretending he hadn't heard.
D He ignored his grandfather despite feeling upset about the criticism.

35 In the fifth paragraph, what is suggested about Rex's attitude to his grandfather?

A Rex has always felt the need to compete with his grandfather.
B Rex believes his grandfather exaggerates his past achievements.
C Rex is sad about the way his relationship with his grandfather has changed.
D Rex feels guilty because he is already more successful than his grandfather was.

36 At the end of the passage, what are we told about Rex?

A He is receiving support to go on an exciting trip.
B He trains regularly whatever the weather is like.
C He gets little encouragement from his mother.
D He is planning to move somewhere less cold.

Part 6

You are going to read an article about a ball that can generate electricity. Six sentences have been removed from the article. Choose from the sentences **A–G** the one which fits each gap (**37–42**). There is one extra sentence which you do not need to use.

Mark your answers **on the separate answer sheet.**

Need electricity? Play a game of soccer!

Two inventors have produced a new soccer ball called 'Soccket' that can generate electricity.

Though 25% of the world's population may not have easy access to electricity, we all have access to a source of energy that is currently being wasted – energy released by our bodies when we move around. Two inventors have figured out how to capture this energy and convert it into electricity. The only equipment needed? A Soccket football and the desire to have some fun.

The story behind this amazing invention began at an unusual engineering class where non-engineers were challenged to combine art and science, and come up with a practical solution to help the world. Two students – Julia Silverman and Jessica Mathews – decided to give it a try. The pair discussed issues facing many people around the world to see which of them they could help tackle. **37** ______

That's when Julia, who used to play a lot of sports in high school, had a brilliant idea: what if they were able to capture some of the energy that is generated when people play sports? **38** ______ Given its popularity among both young and old all over the world, soccer seemed to be the natural sport of choice, and the ball the perfect thing to do it with!

The innovative idea won their professor's approval. It then became the passion and life goal of these two young women. After graduating, they founded Uncharted Play, Inc., a non-profit-making company. **39** ______

They tried their idea out at home first by sticking a shake-to-charge flashlight they had bought inside a small, hollow ball. Then they kicked it around to see if the flashlight would pick up the charge. **40** ______ A mechanism inside the ball captured the energy created as the ball moved, which could then be converted into electricity. They made a number of these balls which were tested by delighted kids at the World Cup Soccer Championships. Just under 150g heavier than a regulation soccer ball, the Soccket had the capacity to store enough energy to power up a small lamp for three hours following just 30 minutes of play.

The company then worked on the first Soccket football to be produced in large numbers. The latest model is six to seven times more energy efficient than the original, and has the capacity to store enough energy to power a reading lamp, a cell phone charger and even a water purifier. **41** ______ The company encourages people not only to buy one for themselves but also to donate one to a country where it might be needed.

And the Soccket is not the young entrepreneurs' only idea – having succeeded with the Soccket, they have many similar ideas combining fun and function. **42** ______ As Silverman says: 'Just because we get older doesn't mean we have to stop playing, and just because we need important things in our life, like electricity, doesn't mean we can't have fun producing them.'

A The version they produced after that was a little more sophisticated.

B Of course, they plan to develop these.

C In this way, the ball could produce even more electricity.

D Maybe they could convert it into electricity.

E Access to cheap electricity was one that came to mind right away.

F This was the first version to become available worldwide.

G They hoped it would help to improve many people's lives.

Part 7

You are going to read four reviews of school concerts. For questions **43–52**, choose from the reviews (**A–D**). The reviews may be chosen more than once.

Mark your answers **on the separate answer sheet**.

Which review writer

is looking forward to hearing the players on another occasion?	**43**	
heard some popular pieces performed in a modern way?	**44**	
says a performance involved a risk that paid off?	**45**	
says a performance was as good as people thought it would be?	**46**	
predicts successful careers for some performers?	**47**	
says the students played more difficult pieces than they normally do?	**48**	
mentions how hard everybody worked before the concert?	**49**	
was impressed by the performers' ability to concentrate?	**50**	
admits that some of the music didn't appeal to them?	**51**	
wishes one performance had been longer?	**52**	

School concert reviews

A Garston High School

Garston High School's annual concert took place in the sports hall last Wednesday. The enthusiasm of the players and their teachers, combined with many hours of rehearsals, produced a varied and enjoyable show, as it does every year. The concert opened with the Garston High School Orchestra, whose expert playing lived up to all expectations. They were followed by the school choir with a dynamic performance of the song, 'Going Places', complete with hand claps, that was much appreciated. Janie Evans' flute solo provided a quiet, peaceful moment, rapidly followed by the choir again with contemporary versions of several well-known favourites. Garston's jazz band then took to the stage, and the audience were soon tapping their feet happily to the lively rhythms. The concert ended with the orchestra in a final inspiring performance. All in all, it was a thoroughly enjoyable evening.

B Hartisford School

Hartisford School's music department has never been regarded as anything special, but after last night's concert that may all be about to change. The college orchestra, unlike in previous years, performed music that challenged musicians, moving away from the more traditional pieces parents and families have become used to. Although at times this proved slightly too ambitious, they deserve credit for trying to aim high. Some of the solo pieces went on for a little too long, but others were entertaining. The students have some hard work to do, but they will no doubt be helped by the new staff at Hartisford. I'm making sure I don't miss their end-of-year concert which I know will be well worth going to.

C Ruttler's School

Some of the students currently attending Ruttler's School are remarkably talented musicians, and it was a pleasure to be in the audience at their concert on Friday. The first solo performance was by Dan Smith, a talented pianist who also played the violin in the orchestra. Next came Emma Jordan on drums, who was brave enough to perform a fast-moving modern piece which even very accomplished professionals might hesitate to play in public. The audience rewarded her by clapping and cheering for several minutes, which she thoroughly deserved. The musicians in the school rock band were on excellent form, though they did play a few numbers that weren't entirely to my taste. The concert finished with all the performers and their teachers on stage at once, playing 'Gotta Go', which was the perfect end to the evening.

D Summerford School

Summerford School's spring concert yesterday was a great success, despite irritating interruptions from mobile phones. The players and singers are to be congratulated for not allowing this to interfere with the performance. The tightly-packed programme gave students an opportunity to show off the range of their talent, and there were so many excellent performances that it would be impossible for me to list them all here. Sarah Liddell on guitar, however, deserves a mention. I was disappointed when her solo ended, as I'd been looking forward to hearing her play. Liam Hunter's piano playing was also outstanding. Another highlight was the string quartet, featuring four very talented young people who will no doubt achieve great things one day. Once again, Summerford School has provided a fantastic evening's entertainment.

WRITING (1 hour 20 minutes)

Part 1

You **must** answer this question. Write your answer in **140–190** words in an appropriate style.

---

1 In your English class you have been comparing large and small schools. Now your English teacher has asked you to write an essay for homework.

Write your essay using **all** the notes and giving reasons for your point of view.

Is it better to go to a large school or a small school?

Notes

Write about:

1. studying and learning

2. making friends

3. .... (your own idea)

Part 2

Write an answer to **one** of the questions **2–5** in this part. Write your answer in **140–190** words in an appropriate style **on the separate answer sheet**. Put the question number in the box at the top of the answer sheet.

---

2 You see this announcement in your school magazine.

> **Articles wanted**
>
> **Finding time to keep fit and healthy**
>
> How do you manage to keep fit and healthy as well as study and spend time with your friends?
>
> Write an article telling us what you think. Write about the food you eat, the exercise you take, and anything else you think is important.
>
> The best articles will be published in next month's school magazine.

Write your **article**.

3 You have received this email from your Australian friend, Sarah.

> We're doing a project in our class about where young people in different countries go for their holidays. Where do **you** usually go for your holidays and what do you do there? Do you enjoy this kind of holiday?
>
> Thanks for your help!
>
> Sarah

Write your **email**.

4 You recently saw this notice in an English-language magazine for teenagers.

> **Reviews wanted**
>
> **A Good Café to Meet Friends in!**
>
> We're doing a guide about cafés where teenagers can go to meet friends and relax. Tell us about a café you know. Write about where it is, the kind of food it serves and the atmosphere there. Tell us why you think other people your age would like it.
>
> The best reviews will be published next month.

Write your **review**.

5 Answer the following question based on the title below.

Touching the Void by Joe Simpson

Your English book club is looking for reviews of adventure stories. Write a review of *Touching the Void*, saying why you would recommend it.

Write your **review**.

LISTENING (approximately 40 minutes)

Part 1

You will hear people talking in eight different situations. For questions **1–8**, choose the best answer (**A**, **B** or **C**).

---

1 You hear a teacher talking to some students.
What is he doing?

A explaining the benefits of walking holidays

B emphasising the natural beauty of some places

C describing the difference between two areas

2 You hear two friends talking about a bike race they went on.
What does the girl say about it?

A She was disappointed with her speed.

B She found it more difficult than expected.

C She almost gave up before the finish.

3 You hear a man and his daughter talking in a library.
What is the man doing?

A recommending a book for his daughter to read

B complaining about his daughter's reading habits

C promising to help his daughter to choose a book

4 You hear two friends talking about a television programme about polar bears.
What do they both think was unusual about it?

A the information given in it

B the location chosen for it

C the skill involved in filming it

5 You hear a teacher talking to a class.
What does she want her students to do this week?

A bring some items to school

B find out some information

C make something at home

6 You hear two friends talking about a story-writing competition.
They agree that they will

A each write a story and go in for it.

B share the prize if one of them wins it.

C visit a zoo together to get ideas for it.

7 You hear a radio announcement about an event.
What is the aim of the event?

A to encourage young people to get involved in science

B to raise city residents' awareness of unusual wildlife

C to find out about trends in animal numbers

8 You hear a review of a computer game on the radio.
What does the reviewer think of the game?

A It is surprisingly different from other adventure games.

B It is likely to have a very broad appeal to computer gamers.

C It is only suitable for people experienced in this type of game.

Part 2

You will hear a girl called Kate giving a class presentation on the subject of chocolate. For questions **9–18**, complete the sentences with a word or short phrase.

Chocolate

Hundreds of years ago, people known as the Mayans added hot peppers and

[**9**] to cocoa beans to make the first chocolate drink.

Kate explains that ancient Mayan people started growing cocoa trees in

[**10**] as chocolate became popular in their culture.

The Aztecs used cocoa beans rather than [**11**]

to settle their debts.

Kate mentions that Spanish explorers brought the [**12**]

to Europe before the cocoa bean.

In the 17th century, the [**13**]

was introduced to protect people's clothes when they drank chocolate.

In 1795, an English company called J. Fry and Sons invented a machine driven by

[**14**] which was used to grind the cocoa beans.

A special machine for making solid chocolate called a [**15**]

was developed in 1828.

In 1847, chocolate [**16**]

began to be produced by an English company.

In 1875, a man from Switzerland called Daniel Peter added

[**17**] to chocolate.

Recent research shows that chocolate can improve people's

[**18**] .

Part 3

You will hear five short extracts in which teenagers are talking about a family day out at an activity centre. For questions **19–23**, choose from the list (**A–H**) what each speaker says about the place they went to. Use the letters only once. There are three extra letters which you do not need to use.

A I bought something useful at the shop.

B I've been given a good reason to go back regularly.

C I enjoy the idea of being independent of my parents.

D I didn't need to take advantage of the help that was available.

E I was able to practise a skill I've been learning elsewhere.

F I didn't manage to do everything I wanted to do.

G I'd be keen to find out more about the place.

H I'd like to do the same activity somewhere nearer home.

Speaker 1		**19**
Speaker 2		**20**
Speaker 3		**21**
Speaker 4		**22**
Speaker 5		**23**

Part 4

You will hear an interview with a girl called Poppy Wallace, who sings in a girl band called GirlSong. For questions **24–30**, choose the best answer (**A**, **B** or **C**).

---

24 What does Poppy say about the band's success this year?

A The girls didn't expect it to happen so quickly.

B The girls haven't had enough time to appreciate it.

C The girls recognise that it was the result of years of hard work.

25 How does Poppy feel about GirlSong's recent tour?

A glad to have spent time with the fans

B pleased that it's made them more confident performers

C happy with the way relationships within the band have developed

26 How did GirlSong come to work with the singer called Leo?

A Their agent contacted him about it.

B He suggested it after hearing their music.

C They met him by chance at a recording studio.

27 What is Poppy's attitude to working with Leo again?

A She's alarmed about the attention they will get.

B She's excited about the opportunity to perform with him.

C She's concerned about the pressure involved.

28 On international tours, Poppy likes to

A make time for seeing the local sights.

B try singing local folk songs.

C learn simple phrases in the local language.

29 What does Poppy enjoy most when she visits Barbados?

A eating the island's food

B playing music with friends

C relaxing on the beach

30 Who did Poppy admire most as a child?

A a singer whose songs she identified with

B a teacher whose lessons inspired her

C a film character whose behaviour appealed to her

SPEAKING (14 minutes)

You take the Speaking test with another candidate (possibly two candidates), referred to here as your partner. There are two examiners. One will speak to you and your partner and the other will be listening. Both examiners will award marks.

Part 1 (2 minutes)

The examiner asks you and your partner questions about yourselves. You may be asked about things like 'your home town', 'your interests', 'your career plans', etc.

Part 2 (a one-minute 'long turn' for each candidate, plus a 20-second response from the second candidate)

The examiner gives you two photographs and asks you to talk about them for one minute. The examiner then asks your partner a question about your photographs and your partner responds briefly.

Then the examiner gives your partner two different photographs. Your partner talks about these photographs for one minute. This time the examiner asks you a question about your partner's photographs and you respond briefly.

Part 3 (4 minutes)

The examiner asks you and your partner to talk together. You may be asked to solve a problem or try to come to a decision about something. For example, you might be asked to decide the best way to use some rooms in a language school. The examiner gives you some text to help you but does not join in the conversation.

Part 4 (4 minutes)

The examiner asks some further questions, which leads to a more general discussion of what you have talked about in Part 3. You may comment on your partner's answers if you wish.

Test 3

READING AND USE OF ENGLISH (1 hour 15 minutes)

Part 1

For questions **1–8**, read the text below and decide which answer (**A**, **B**, **C** or **D**) best fits each gap. There is an example at the beginning (**0**).

Mark your answers **on the separate answer sheet**.

Example:

0 **A** trying **B** doing **C** finding **D** carrying

0	A	B	C	D
	▬	▭	▭	▭

Testing games

How lucky can you be? Twelve-year-old Eloise Noakes has got the best job in the world – **(0)** .... out new games. A **(1)** .... company held a competition to find young testers and Eloise was selected to test games which are about to be **(2)** .... onto the market. Each week she is given a different game to play before **(3)** .... her thoughts on a form designed by the company. As the company director said, 'What better way to find out about games than to put them in the hands of the customers who will make most **(4)** .... of them?' Eloise is **(5)** .... with her new job but she also takes it very **(6)** .... She is allowed to keep the games after testing them, but she has decided instead to give them **(7)** .... to children less fortunate than herself. 'I've got **(8)** .... of games and some children don't have any,' she explained.

	A	B	C	D
1	**A** primary	**B** chief	**C** superior	**D** leading
2	**A** sold	**B** launched	**C** promoted	**D** sent
3	**A** signing	**B** copying	**C** recording	**D** filling
4	**A** use	**B** value	**C** practice	**D** worth
5	**A** amused	**B** delighted	**C** thankful	**D** proud
6	**A** calmly	**B** deeply	**C** thoroughly	**D** seriously
7	**A** back	**B** over	**C** away	**D** in
8	**A** plenty	**B** many	**C** enough	**D** several

Part 2

For questions **9–16**, read the text below and think of the word which best fits each gap. Use only **one** word in each gap. There is an example at the beginning (**0**).

Write your answers **IN CAPITAL LETTERS on the separate answer sheet**.

Example: | 0 | O N E |

Reading is good for you

Reading really is **(0)** .... of the best hobbies you can have. **(9)** .... only is it entertaining, but it also improves your mind; when you're reading, you're frequently having **(10)** .... work things out, so you're actively using your brain. And you often come **(11)** .... new words, so it's good for improving your vocabulary too.

Another benefit of reading is that it develops your memory. If you're reading detective fiction, for example, you'll find **(12)** .... hard to follow the story **(13)** .... you can remember all the little details which are essential to the plot. Moreover, people who read a lot tend to **(14)** .... more imaginative because they're exposed to new ideas, and this helps to develop the creative side of the brain. It might also boost your confidence because reading can increase your general knowledge – you'll always have **(15)** .... interesting to talk about! So what are you waiting for? **(16)** .... reading a try!

Part 3

For questions **17–24**, read the text below. Use the word given in capitals at the end of some of the lines to form a word that fits in the gap **in the same line**. There is an example at the beginning (**0**).

Write your answers **IN CAPITAL LETTERS on the separate answer sheet.**

Example: | 0 | S O C I E T Y |

Outward Bound

Have you ever wanted to hike up a mountain, sleep in a boat or spend a	
day completely cut off from modern **(0)** .... , but didn't because you	**SOCIAL**
were **(17)** .... to give it a try? Well, now you can turn your dreams	**FRIGHT**
into reality on an Outward Bound programme. We run courses all over	
the world which are designed to improve people's **(18)** .... of the	**KNOW**
great outdoors and to experience things that it would be **(19)** .... to	**POSSIBLE**
experience in their **(20)** .... lives. But an Outward Bound course is	**DAY**
not only about adventure, it is a journey of **(21)** .... , during which	**DISCOVER**
you learn about yourself and others. The activities teach you valuable	
lessons about your own strengths and **(22)** .... and along the way	**WEAK**
you will form many new **(23)** .... The days you spend on an Outward	**FRIEND**
Bound course will help you to find out who you really are and what you	
want to be. So why not join us? It could be one of the best **(24)**	**DECIDE**
you will ever make!	

Part 4

For questions **25–30**, complete the second sentence so that it has a similar meaning to the first sentence, using the word given. **Do not change the word given**. You must use between **two** and **five** words, including the word given. Here is an example (**0**).

Example:

0 Prizes are given out when the school year finishes.

PLACE

Prize-giving .... end of each school year.

The gap can be filled by the words 'takes place at the', so you write:

Example:	**0**	*TAKES PLACE AT THE*

Write **only** the missing words **IN CAPITAL LETTERS on the separate answer sheet.**

---

25 It's a pity I didn't see Jane before she went on holiday.

WISH

I .... Jane before she went on holiday.

26 Richard only arrived just before the concert began.

TURN

Richard .... until just before the concert began.

27 Despite not feeling well, Lisa went to the cinema with her friends.

ALTHOUGH

Lisa went to the cinema with her friends .... well.

28 When does the bus leave on Sundays?

WHAT

Can you tell me .... on Sundays?

29 This computer package includes all the software.

INCLUDED

All the software .... this computer package.

30 My teacher let me leave the lesson early because I wasn't feeling well.

ALLOWED

I .... the lesson early because I wasn't feeling well.

Part 5

You are going to read a magazine article about a young mountain climber. For questions **31–36**, choose the answer (**A**, **B**, **C** or **D**) which you think fits best according to the text.

Mark your answers **on the separate answer sheet.**

Teenage Climber

Kai Bradey is 14 and plans to be one of the youngest people ever to climb Mount Everest. Kai's team for the climb includes his father, Ed, and mother, Melissa. They call themselves 'The Bradey Team', and climbing Everest is only one part of their plan. If Kai succeeds in climbing Everest, and Koscuiszko in Australia, he will become one of the youngest people to have climbed the Seven Summits, the highest points on each continent. Few people achieve this under the age of thirty. Kai has already climbed four of them and might actually do it before his teenage years are over. If he makes it, he could become one of the most famous teens of his generation. Because young people are spending more time on computers and games consoles, Kai hopes to inspire kids to climb their own mountains. Or, at least, to venture outdoors.

I have spoken to a number of well-known Everest climbers and could not find a single one who thought that taking a 14-year-old up the world's highest mountain was a good idea. They questioned whether many young climbers had the necessary physical strength, and had doubts about whether a teenager would be prepared emotionally for the challenge. In addition, they couldn't see how a young person could have gained enough practical knowledge or awareness of potential hazards to develop the good judgment and reactions a climber must have in order to take part in such a project safely.

The Bradeys have heard such views before. 'I know that people are critical of us – I have to put up with that,' Ed says, 'but I don't waste my time thinking about it – there's still so much to do. I think about possible problems, obviously. Melissa and I weigh up the risks all the time. I'm concerned for Kai's safety as any parent would be, but I believe our own backgound as climbers will help, and watching Kai develop gives me confidence.'

I also wonder about Kai's motivation. Is this just an ambitious father taking his own love of adventure to a dangerous extreme? 'This project isn't about me trying to become famous for my son's achievements,' Ed insists. 'At first, he talked about it as something for later in life, but when we discussed it, we thought: 'Why wait?' We talk to him from time to time to make sure he hasn't lost the motivation to do it.' When I ask Kai what pleasure he finds in the challenge he says, 'I just focus on achieving my goal.'

In the past, few knew or cared about being the youngest or fastest person to climb a particular mountain, or sail a particular ocean. Today, every adventure is blogged about, and every climb turns into a record-setting challenge. The more adventurous the record, the more interest it generates. This gives Kai a dilemma. We may complain that achievement too often replaces enjoyment during such challenges, but if Kai wants to inspire others, he has got to play the media game. This means blogging, sitting for photo shoots and giving interviews. He has got to offer something truly spectacular. Like climbing Everest. 'And in fact,' Ed says. 'If Kai decides next week that he's had enough of mountain climbing and wants to swim instead, we'll forget about this whole project and go to the pool.'

31 In the first paragraph, we learn that Kai's aim is

A to persuade teenagers to exercise more.
B to become a very well-known person.
C to encourage teenagers to join him on his expedition.
D to give people a better impression of teenagers.

32 What does 'it' refer to in line 12 ?

A climbing five of the Seven Summits
B being the youngest person to climb Everest
C climbing Mount Everest and Koscuiszko
D completing the Seven Summits climbs

33 The experienced climbers that the writer spoke to think that

A mountain climbing is an unsuitable activity for some teenagers.
B mountain climbing can help teenagers to develop emotionally.
C teenagers lack the climbing experience needed to make certain decisions.
D teenagers are not physically strong enough for mountain climbing.

34 What do we find out about Ed in the third paragraph?

A He has difficulty dealing with the criticism of others.
B He wonders whether Kai needs more climbing experience.
C He has considered the dangers involved in the expedition.
D He is worried about running out of time to prepare.

35 What is suggested in the fourth paragraph?

A Ed will use the expedition to find fame.
B Kai is genuinely interested in climbing Everest.
C The family should leave the expedition until Kai is older.
D There is little communication between Kai and his parents.

36 What is the writer's attitude towards Kai in the fifth paragraph?

A He recognises that Kai needs to do something that attracts attention.
B He criticises the fact that Kai is only interested in breaking records.
C He thinks Kai is unwilling to work with the media.
D He believes Kai should do something even more challenging.

Part 6

You are going to read an article about the invention of roller coasters. Six sentences have been removed from the article. Choose from the sentences **A–G** the one which fits each gap (**37–42**). There is one extra sentence which you do not need to use.

Mark your answers **on the separate answer sheet.**

The history of roller coasters

Roller coasters have a long history, and although most of them are now found in the USA, their origins lie elsewhere.

As early as the 15th century, a popular pastime for Russians was sliding down snow-covered hills on a sledge, much as children still do during the winter in many countries today. **37** ____ These consisted of a wooden slope covered in ice, on top of a wooden frame. Riders sat on large blocks of ice, and the slides, which could be up to 24 metres high, became so popular that even the royal family were said to be fans.

Soldiers returning to France from Russia are thought to have taken with them stories of the 'Russian mountains', and variations of the Russian slides began to appear in France. To make up for the lack of snow and ice, the slides had wooden tracks along which people rode in small cars with wheels. **38** ____ Such freedom of movement meant that they often bumped into each other.

This all changed in 1817, with the opening, in Paris, of two new slides or 'roller coasters', which had cars that were secured to the tracks. Thanks to this improvement, they were now much safer to ride in, which, in turn, meant that they could go faster. **39** ____ However, in 1826 a mechanical system was introduced to drag them up to the start of the ride again.

The following year, a mining company in the USA constructed a railway in Pennsylvania to carry coal in similar small cars from the mine, which was situated at the top of a mountain, to the canal at the bottom.

From there, it could be put on boats. **40** ____ The return trip, however, involved a team of donkeys pulling the cars back up, and took six times as long. In order to solve this problem, a second track was built so that steam engines could be used to do this.

In 1872, with the mine now closed, the railway became a tourist attraction. Visitors came from miles around to travel to the top of the mountain, enjoy the views, and then take the railway down again. **41** ____

One of the passengers on the railway, Marcus Thompson, saw the potential of such an experience, and decided to construct what we now recognise as the first roller coaster. It opened in 1884 at Coney Island in New York, and was an instant success. Thompson charged 5 cents a ride, and earned his entire investment back in just a few days, such was the popularity of this new ride. By the end of the century, roller coasters could be found at funfairs across the country. **42** ____ It is a battle that continues to this day.

A This was built the opposite way around, so that the cars were initially pulled to the top of the slope and then dropped down very suddenly.

B Initially, people had to be employed for the tough job of pushing them back to the top.

C These were not locked in place as they are today, so they tended to slip in all directions as they went down.

D It was this last part of the ride that was memorable as the cars travelled at great speed and round several tight corners.

E Within two hundred years, man-made versions were common in the flatter areas of the country.

F As more and more were built, the need to attract customers meant that manufacturers began to compete to create ever more exhilarating rides.

G The journey involved transporting the load down a steep hill for 14 kilometres and could be completed in only 30 minutes.

Part 7

You are going to read a magazine article in which four teenagers talk about their experiences of taking part in a reality TV series, which aims to find the best young business person. For questions **43–52**, choose from the people (**A–D**). The people may be chosen more than once.

Mark your answers **on the separate answer sheet**.

Which person

learnt that academic ability is not necessary for doing well in business?	**43**	
says they have a competitive nature?	**44**	
was determined to enjoy their experience on the show?	**45**	
discovered that winning the show was not as easy as they had thought?	**46**	
believes you should go into business with people who have similar ambitions?	**47**	
thinks you need a variety of skills to succeed in business?	**48**	
says that if you want success you have to work hard?	**49**	
wanted to change the image of a certain group of people?	**50**	
says the show taught them to appreciate different styles of working?	**51**	
says you should not listen to those who doubt you?	**52**	

Young business people

A Zoe, 17 years old

I applied to do it because I wanted to show off my talent for business and maybe persuade someone to hire me. I'm a keen viewer of the show, and I'd always wanted to appear on it as I felt I'd be a very strong candidate. I'm the kind of person who won't be beaten, so I felt that the show would be an ideal environment for me. It was exhausting, but also rewarding and fun. I enjoyed all the tasks we had to do. Having had this experience, my advice to other young business people would be: know what you want to do, be creative and decisive and you'll fulfil your potential. Personally, I've learnt that there are all kinds of people in business; it's important to be tolerant of the various ways that people do things, and to value each individual, because everyone has something to offer.

B Kirsty, 16 years old

As I'm a big fan of the show, it was great to have the opportunity to appear on it. I thought it would be a brilliant way to see how far I could go in the competition and get a taste of working in business. I had the time of my life – it's the best thing I've ever done! I think the experience has made me more confident in my strengths. I'm not that good at some of the stuff we study at school, but I realise now that, with enough determination, I can get to where I want to be in this environment. To anyone hoping to get into business at a young age, stay focused on your goals, and don't be put off by constantly being told what you can't achieve. I've learnt that you have to co-operate in business, and that the work of a team is always more successful than that of an individual.

C Tim, 18 years old

When the opportunity came up to take part in the show, I just couldn't turn it down. I've always been a fan. Like everyone who watches at home, I always believed I could outdo everyone else – until I was actually there and found out what was expected of me! I loved every minute though. It really made me grow up. I've learned that in the business world a broad range of abilities is necessary to really get on; it's not enough to be very good in just one area. I advise young business people to make sure they put enough effort in if they are to achieve their goals. Natural ability is important of course, but it's not enough on its own.

D Arjun, 17 years old

I applied for the show because I thought it would give me the opportunity to demonstrate that academics don't just sit and study books all day. Also, I thought it would allow me to learn more about business. I knew that I'd never have the chance to do something like that again so I decided to make the most of every second. Obviously, winning was fantastic, but I think that meeting all those different people during the competition was the real highlight for me. To young businessmen and women, I'd say: never give up on your dreams. If you believe in yourself then anything is possible. From taking part in this show, I've learnt it's vital to join forces with others who share your objectives and that the success of a business depends on the team that's running it and their passion towards whatever it is that's being sold.

WRITING (1 hour 20 minutes)

Part 1

You must answer this question. Write your answer in **140–190** words in an appropriate style.

---

1 In your English class you have been talking about playing computer games. Now your English teacher has asked you to write an essay for homework.

Write your essay using **all** the notes and giving reasons for your point of view.

'Playing computer games is a complete waste of time.' Do you agree?

Notes

Write about:

1. what you can learn by playing computer games
2. what you can do instead of playing computer games
3. .... (your own idea)

Part 2

Write an answer to one of the questions **2–5** in this part. Write your answer in **140–190** words in an appropriate style **on the separate answer sheet**. Put the question number in the box at the top of the answer sheet.

---

2 You see this announcement in an English-language magazine for teenagers.

> **Articles wanted**
>
> **What makes a perfect school?**
>
> Write an article telling us what **you** think. Write about the teachers, the lessons, the building and anything else you think is important.
>
> We will publish the best articles in next month's magazine.

Write your **article**.

3 You recently saw this notice on an English-language website called *Teen Fun*.

> **Reviews wanted**
>
> **A Great Place to Go**
>
> We're looking for reviews of places that young people enjoy going to. It could be a theme park, a leisure centre, a club or somewhere else.
>
> Tell us about a place you go to, what you can do there, and what you like most about it.
>
> The best reviews will be put on our website next month.

Write your **review**.

4 You have seen this announcement in an international magazine for teenagers.

> **Stories wanted**
>
> We are looking for stories for our new English-language magazine for teenagers. Your story must **begin** with this sentence: *Robert was excited as he jumped into the boat.*
>
> Your story must include:
>
> - an escape
> - a cave

Write your **story**.

5 Answer the following question based on the title below.

Touching the Void by Joe Simpson

You see this announcement in your school English magazine:

> **Articles wanted**
>
> We are looking for articles about friendship in the book *Touching the Void.*
> How important is friendship in the story?
> How does the friendship between Joe and Simon change?

Write your **article**.

LISTENING (approximately 40 minutes)

Part 1

You will hear people talking in eight different situations. For questions **1–8**, choose the best answer (**A**, **B** or **C**).

---

1 You hear a girl who is going to live in another country talking to a friend.
They agree that it will be

A exciting to live in a new place.

B easy to make new friends.

C simple to keep in touch.

2 You hear part of a science programme about a planned space mission to the moons of Jupiter.
Why does the presenter regard them as a good place to explore?

A Something could be living there.

B There's a lot of volcanic activity there.

C It will show how far it's possible to travel.

3 You hear a girl telling her father about a writer who visited her school.
What did she think about the writer?

A She was pleased to meet him because she enjoys his books.

B She was surprised to find out how many books he's written.

C She was interested to learn about what inspires him.

4 You hear part of an interview with a girl who is talking about some wolves she saw.
How did the girl feel when she saw the second wolf?

A less afraid than she would have expected

B sorry that she was unable to photograph it

C grateful that she lives in such an exciting place

5 You hear a young racing driver talking on the radio.
What is the speaker's main purpose?

A to outline the advantages and disadvantages of his sport

B to explain what it takes to be a successful racing driver

C to inform listeners about his own background in racing

6 You overhear a boy talking about a football competition he has been in.
How does he feel?

A exhausted because of the pressure

B enthusiastic at getting so far

C upset because his team didn't win

7 You overhear a girl talking about a club she has recently started going to.
What does she say about it?

A It's not what she expected.

B She doesn't enjoy everything about it.

C She has learnt a lot since joining.

8 You hear a teacher talking to her class about some homework they did.
What do the class need to do better in future assignments?

A organise their work clearly

B label visuals appropriately

C check their work carefully

Part 2

You will hear a student called Emily giving a class presentation about a whale watching trip she went on with her family. For questions **9–18**, complete the sentences with a word or short phrase.

Whale watching

The guide on Emily's trip spends most of his time working as a [**9**] .

At first, Emily found it difficult to tell the difference between a [**10**] and a whale.

Emily says that the guides used a [**11**] to communicate with each other.

The fact that many whales have no [**12**] was one thing that surprised Emily.

It's possible to find out the age of a whale by looking at something inside its [**13**] .

Emily thought that the [**14**] of the first whale she saw was an unusual colour.

Emily says that the large whale she saw was similar to a [**15**] in shape.

To protect the whales, boats have to stay more than [**16**] metres away from them.

Emily advises anyone who goes whale watching to take a [**17**] with them.

Emily and her family were lucky enough to see [**18**] near to the coast.

Part 3

You will hear five short extracts in which teenagers are talking about a new video game. For questions **19–23**, choose from the list (**A–H**) the opinion each speaker expresses. Use the letters only once. There are three extra letters which you do not need to use.

A It's less exciting than a previous version of the same game.

B The special effects were what made me interested in it.

C The pace of it is rather slow.

D It gives players some interesting choices to make.

E At first, it's difficult to understand what you have to do.

F It's likely to appeal to a different age group.

G The later levels introduce some unusual elements.

H My friend's better at it than I am.

Speaker 1		**19**
Speaker 2		**20**
Speaker 3		**21**
Speaker 4		**22**
Speaker 5		**23**

Part 4

You will hear an interview with Jack Herbert, a talented young pianist. For questions **24–30**, choose the best answer (**A**, **B** or **C**).

---

24 When Jack was a child, his grandmother

A gave him his first lessons on the piano.

B sometimes disagreed with his piano teacher.

C helped him when he found learning the piano difficult.

25 What does Jack say about other members of his family?

A His brother no longer performs in public.

B His parents have both played professionally.

C His sister makes her living as a musician.

26 How did Jack feel during his time at the National Music School?

A pleased to have the opportunity to be there

B worried that he wouldn't live up to expectations

C frustrated that he couldn't choose which pieces to play

27 What is Jack's attitude to practising?

A He doesn't take it as seriously as he used to.

B He feels it's essential for good performance.

C He wishes he didn't have to do so much of it.

28 When he's performing in a live concert, Jack aims to

A interpret the music in his own way.

B share his enjoyment of the music with others.

C play the music better than he's ever done before.

29 Jack thinks that he's different to other pianists of his age because

A he plays a wider range of musical styles.

B he brings classical music up to date.

C he appeals to a young audience.

30 What does Jack plan to do in the future?

A travel more widely

B compose more of his own music

C enter big music competitions

SPEAKING (14 minutes)

You take the Speaking test with another candidate (possibly two candidates), referred to here as your partner. There are two examiners. One will speak to you and your partner and the other will be listening. Both examiners will award marks.

Part 1 (2 minutes)

The examiner asks you and your partner questions about yourselves. You may be asked about things like 'your home town', 'your interests', 'your career plans', etc.

Part 2 (a one-minute 'long turn' for each candidate, plus a 20-second response from the second candidate)

The examiner gives you two photographs and asks you to talk about them for one minute. The examiner then asks your partner a question about your photographs and your partner responds briefly.

Then the examiner gives your partner two different photographs. Your partner talks about these photographs for one minute. This time the examiner asks you a question about your partner's photographs and you respond briefly.

Part 3 (4 minutes)

The examiner asks you and your partner to talk together. You may be asked to solve a problem or try to come to a decision about something. For example, you might be asked to decide the best way to use some rooms in a language school. The examiner gives you some text to help you but does not join in the conversation.

Part 4 (4 minutes)

The examiner asks some further questions, which leads to a more general discussion of what you have talked about in Part 3. You may comment on your partner's answers if you wish.

Test 4

READING AND USE OF ENGLISH (1 hour 15 minutes)

Part 1

For questions **1–8**, read the text below and decide which answer (**A**, **B**, **C** or **D**) best fits each gap. There is an example at the beginning (**0**).

Mark your answers **on the separate answer sheet**.

Example:

0 **A** getting **B** coming **C** setting **D** putting

0	A	B	C	D
	▬	▭	▭	▭

Cycling holidays

Some of my best holidays have involved **(0)** .... around on two wheels, cycling through the countryside with my family. Our **(1)** .... is for off-road trails where there is no need to worry about other traffic and we can **(2)** .... our time, cycling at our own speed and **(3)** .... for a while to have a rest and **(4)** .... the view. The best routes are away from the crowds but within easy **(5)** .... of accommodation and eating places. Cycling holidays take little planning; we just pick a route, pack essential clothing and set off. Because we have to carry everything with us all the time, we are very strict about what we take – so that **(6)** .... nothing heavy. If you fancy **(7)** .... this a try yourself, there are lots of books and websites that will help you plan a route. There are even companies that will **(8)** .... you with all the equipment you need. So get on your bike and start exploring!

1	**A**	preference	**B**	alternative	**C**	favourite	**D**	option
2	**A**	make	**B**	take	**C**	leave	**D**	catch
3	**A**	waiting	**B**	hesitating	**C**	delaying	**D**	pausing
4	**A**	admire	**B**	regard	**C**	grasp	**D**	observe
5	**A**	distance	**B**	reach	**C**	length	**D**	range
6	**A**	causes	**B**	results	**C**	means	**D**	leads
7	**A**	doing	**B**	making	**C**	having	**D**	giving
8	**A**	offer	**B**	lend	**C**	provide	**D**	recommend

Part 2

For questions **9–16**, read the text below and think of the word which best fits each gap. Use only **one** word in each gap. There is an example at the beginning (**0**).

Write your answers **IN CAPITAL LETTERS on the separate answer sheet**.

Example: | 0 | | W | H | A | T |

Food in space

Have you ever wondered **(0)** .... astronauts eat while they're in space? Well, currently there's not a great deal of choice because making space food is far more difficult than anyone **(9)** .... imagine. The food absolutely **(10)** .... to be nutritious because astronauts' bodies are put under a lot of pressure. They need food in **(11)** .... to maintain their energy levels and keep their spirits up. So scientists are looking for volunteers to help them work **(12)** ....how to improve the quality and choice of food for future space missions. The volunteers will experience exactly what life is **(13)** .... for real astronauts by living inside a fake space capsule and wearing spacesuits. They will spend 120 days living on nothing **(14)** .... space food, recording **(15)** .... time it takes to prepare it, **(16)** .... good it tastes and whether their food choices change over time. At the end of the project, the scientists hope to come up with exciting new food solutions for the astronauts of the future.

Part 3

For questions **17–24**, read the text below. Use the word given in capitals at the end of some of the lines to form a word that fits in the gap **in the same line**. There is an example at the beginning (**0**).

Write your answers **IN CAPITAL LETTERS on the separate answer sheet.**

Example: | 0 | V | I | L | L | A | G | E | R | S |

Ancient writing

In 1999, **(0)** .... in the state of Velacruz, in Mexico, uncovered a stone	**VILLAGE**
block with marks carved onto its surface. **(17)** .... archaeologists	**MEXICO**
realised how important the marks were: the patterns covering the stone	
seemed to provide **(18)** .... of a system of writing based on pictures	**EVIDENT**
and symbols. The find was particularly **(19)** .... because it was the	**EXCITE**
oldest example of writing ever found in the region.	
The **(20)** .... patterns, or 'hieroglyphics', include fascinating images	**REMARK**
of snakes and birds. Most experts are aware of the **(21)** .... of the	**SIGNIFICANT**
find, but there is still some **(22)** .... about who wrote the ancient	**AGREE**
message. It is hoped that other similar **(23)** .... in the future will	**DISCOVER**
give researchers a greater degree of certainty about the origins of the	
symbols. Experts **(24)** .... believe they were written by a civilisation	**GENERAL**
known as the Olmecs.	

Part 4

For questions **25–30**, complete the second sentence so that it has a similar meaning to the first sentence, using the word given. **Do not change the word given**. You must use between **two** and **five** words, including the word given. Here is an example (**0**).

Example:

0 Prizes are given out when the school year finishes.

PLACE

Prize-giving .... end of each school year.

The gap can be filled by the words 'takes place at the', so you write:

Example:	**0**	*TAKES PLACE AT THE*

Write **only** the missing words **IN CAPITAL LETTERS on the separate answer sheet**.

---

25 Wear some warm clothes because it might get cold later.

CASE

Wear some warm clothes .... cold later.

26 I really regret eating all that chocolate.

WISH

I really .... all that chocolate.

27 'I'm sorry I didn't do my homework,' said Maria.

NOT

Maria apologised .... her homework.

28 I missed the train because I got to the station late.

CAUGHT

If I had got to the station on time, ... the train.

29 Unfortunately, I only realised I'd lost my keys when I arrived home.

UNTIL

Unfortunately, ... I arrived home that I realised I'd lost my keys.

30 I'm sure Simon went home early because I can't see him anywhere.

MUST

Simon .... home early because I can't see him anywhere.

Part 5

You are going to read a magazine article in which a teenager discusses classical music. For questions **31–36**, choose the answer (**A**, **B**, **C** or **D**) which you think fits best according to the text.

Mark your answers **on the separate answer sheet.**

Teenagers and Classical Music

When you see a teenager with an MP3 player, you can be pretty certain it's not classical music they're listening to. Most of us can list the names of dozens of pop groups, but ask any of my friends if they know who Brahms was and you can tell by the expression on their face that they haven't a clue. I have just started doing a music degree, but the people on my course know no more about the works of great composers than anyone else our age. And if you don't know who wrote the music, you are unlikely to go out and buy any recordings of their work.

The statistics must be depressing for a lover of classical music. Apparently only 3% of concert tickets sold last year were for classical music events, and the average classical recording sells a mere 300 copies. I must say I still find that hard to believe. So what has caused this decline in interest for a type of music that has lasted for centuries? The older generation are irritated by our obsession with TV and video games, blaming it for most things, but I don't think there is any connection in this case. The simple truth is that classical music just doesn't hold much attraction for most people, and that is particularly true of teenagers, who are the ones most likely to buy music and concert tickets.

Now I'm aware that this doesn't apply to everyone my age. I know some teenagers who go to classical music concerts all the time, but they are a minority. Although I am a musician and play in an orchestra, I'm not exactly a classical music fan. I enjoy a huge range of styles, but judging by what's stored on my computer, my classical music consumption is probably pretty close to that 3% figure.

So why don't teenagers like classical music? Well, first of all, the pace and rhythm of classical music, with its numerous changes of mood, are problematic for us. We like to talk fast, play fast, and think fast. In addition, if you believe the experts, we have difficulty paying attention for more than about three minutes; far too short for most pieces of classical music, but perfect for a pop song. Pop is structurally quite simple and therefore easy to listen to, while appreciating a piece of classical music requires time and concentration. The subject matter of pop music also holds much more appeal than a lengthy piece of classical music with no lyrics. Classical music is incredibly powerful, but not exactly full of the issues that concern teenagers.

The way we listen to music has also changed. In the past, families would gather at home to make music together, and an ability to play an instrument was highly valued. The only other opportunity to hear music was at a concert. Nowadays, you can find any music you want at the click of a mouse, and yet the sound track to our lives is rarely classical. When did you last go into a shop that had classical music playing in the background?

In my orchestra we play classical music in all sorts of different places, but no matter how cool the posters are, I see virtually nothing but grey hair when I look into the crowd. Some say that the lack of interest in classical music among teenagers is the fault of our schools, but there are plenty of kids eager to play classical music in their school orchestra. They arrive early to practise and stay after school to rehearse. Classical music appeals to them when they perform, but otherwise it is not their music of choice. The two activities have become separated. When we want to relax, it's always pop music.

31 In the first paragraph, what does the writer say about teenagers?

A Their knowledge of classical music is limited to the names of composers.
B They don't listen to classical music because they don't know what to buy.
C Even the ones who study music have limited knowledge of classical music.
D Some would be embarrassed to admit to having classical music on their MP3 player.

32 How does the writer feel about the statistics she mentions in the second paragraph?

A disappointed that people are losing interest in classical music
B annoyed that older people criticise the things that she enjoys
C surprised that so few people buy classical music recordings
D certain that the future of classical music depends on teenagers

33 What is the meaning of 'classical music consumption' in line 34?

A the amount of music she listens to
B the amount of music she plays
C the number of concerts she attends
D the number of recordings she has made

34 The writer believes that teenagers prefer pop music because

A the style of it is always changing.
B the words used in it are relevant to their lives.
C it suits their many changes of mood.
D listening to it helps them to focus.

35 In the fifth paragraph, what does the writer say about classical music?

A We only really enjoyed it at concerts.
B We don't notice it being played.
C We should appreciate the way it is played.
D We hear it less than other kinds of music.

36 What is the writer's main point in the last paragraph?

A Pop music is generally more relaxing to listen to than classical music.
B Those who play classical music often don't like listening to it.
C Good classical musicians usually have to spend a lot of time practising.
D Schools are to blame if teenagers are not interested in classical music.

Part 6

You are going to read an article about Antarctica. Six sentences have been removed from the article. Choose from the sentences **A–G** the one which fits each gap (**37–42**). There is one extra sentence which you do not need to use.

Mark your answers **on the separate answer sheet.**

Rainforest in Antarctica

Scientists have discovered that Antarctica looked very different 55 million years ago!

Antarctica is the fifth largest continent after Asia, Africa, North America and South America. It covers 14 million km^2, 98% of which is ice.

Antarctica is frozen now, but a study has found that there were trees similar to palm trees in the Antarctic 55 million years ago, in a period known as the early Eocene era. **37** ____ Global levels of the principal greenhouse gas, carbon dioxide, were nearly three times as high then as today.

Scientists have known for a long time that the start of the Eocene era was one of the hottest periods in Earth's history, so at that time Antarctica would have been ice free and much warmer than at present. **38** ____

For millions of years, rock, plants and animal bones have been ground down by wind, water and the sheer weight of ice to tiny pieces known as sediment. Scientists have now analysed samples of Antarctic sediment from the Eocene period. These were not available to them until very recently. **39** ____ Unfortunately, any sediment remaining there from the Eocene period was destroyed as Antarctica's climate changed or buried under thousands of metres of ice.

Now technology has allowed researchers to analyse sediment from under the sea. The study was carried out by a team of 36 scientists off the coast of Antarctica. They dropped a drilling machine through 4 km of water, and used it to make a long thin hole, 1 km deep, into the ocean floor. Then a metal tube was pushed down into the sediment to take a sample, and a sort of lid was closed over it. **40** ____ One of the authors of the study said: 'The samples are the first detailed evidence we have of what was happening in the Antarctic during this vitally important era.'

Throughout the Eocene period, tiny pieces of plant were transported by insects, or washed to the bottom of the sea bed just off the coast. They then settled into the sediment and were preserved for 50 million years. **41** ____ Analysis of the plant pieces in the sediment samples reveals that the coast of Antarctica used to be covered in warm rainforest similar to that in northern Australia or New Guinea. Further inland, mountainous regions were covered in different kinds of trees.

This discovery suggests that temperatures on the Antarctic coast were around 16°C and summers reached a pleasant 21°C. Antarctica was in nearly the same position as it is now, over the South Pole. As a result, it would have been dark in winter, like today. **42** ____ Temperatures probably never fell below 10°C.

The vegetation of Antarctica is very different today from 55 million years ago. There are no trees or bushes on the continent, and only two species of flowering plants are found along the western side of the Antarctic Peninsula. What will it be like, though, in another 50 million years?

A The main reason for this is that they had previously only been able to look on land.

B So they decided to collect some more samples in winter, despite the difficulties involved.

C The presence of particular plants, however, indicates that it was fairly warm even during those coldest months.

D They could grow there because at that time the area had a near-tropical climate with frost-free winters, even in the polar darkness.

E Some of them have now been brought up in the tubes.

F But their new findings have provided the first ever detailed information about its environment and, consequently, its climate.

G This ensured it remained inside as it was pulled out.

Part 7

You are going to read an article in which four teenage girls describe school trips they have been on. For questions **43–52**, choose from the people (**A–D**). The people may be chosen more than once.

Mark your answers **on the separate answer sheet.**

Which person

recommends something she did?	**43**	
appreciates having made new friends?	**44**	
regretted a choice she made?	**45**	
was persuaded to do something which proved enjoyable?	**46**	
thought of ideas for group activities?	**47**	
had concerns that were shared by other people?	**48**	
was reassured by a good first impression?	**49**	
is not sure she was told the truth?	**50**	
enjoyed some activities more than other people did?	**51**	
had expected some people to behave differently?	**52**	

School trips

A Lisa

The trip was organised at the beginning of the academic year because we hadn't seen each other much over the summer. It was basically six days doing activities like mountain walking and canoeing. We offered to help with the cooking, which was actually quite good fun. The plan was that we would do things all together in the evenings; my friends and I came up with stuff like games and talent shows, and we even put on a play one night. We performed it for the teachers, who really liked it – at least, that's what they said at the time! It didn't really matter anyway, because we all had such a laugh. Some friends of mine even posted a video of it online when we got home. I hope we can do something like that again some time.

B Rosa

I must admit I expected it to be a bit of a waste of time. This trip was compulsory for the whole class, and I thought it might be dreadful! Anyway, when we got off the train and I saw the lovely village where we were staying, I knew straight away it would be all right. Our teachers were really friendly and did loads of sports with us, which was perfect for me, but not that great for some of my less sporty friends. On one day we could choose to go either to a museum or to an art gallery. I went to the museum, which was a poor decision as the alternative, the art gallery, was pretty cool and everyone should see it apparently. All in all, though, I had a great time and I'll definitely be on the next trip!

C Claire

We were away for three days, and on one of them we visited a huge cave. I was anxious about going underground into the dark! All my friends teased me about that but said I'd be OK and that they'd look after me, so I went along. I didn't like it at all at first, but when I eventually relaxed and started to look around properly, I have to say it was stunning. There were lights along all the paths inside the cave and they'd also put some up so you could see the different rock formations there. So in the end, it wasn't scary at all. The rest of the trip was fun too, but I'd say that was the highlight. I wish I could go back there with my family, but it's too far away. But should you be in that area, it is definitely worth a visit.

D Jana

I hadn't wanted to go on any school trips before because I was worried about being away from my parents. I know it sounds silly, but I also know I wasn't the only one. There was no choice this time; the whole class had to go. It was only for the weekend in any case, and not far from home either. We went camping – luckily, it didn't rain. I thought the teachers might be strict with us, but that wasn't the case at all. We went for long walks in the forest during the day, but probably the best bit was in the evenings when we sat round a campfire in a big circle and sang funny songs. I even ended up getting close to people I'd never talked to much at school before, so the trip really was worthwhile.

WRITING (1 hour 20 minutes)

Part 1

You must answer this question. Write your answer in **140–190** words in an appropriate style.

---

1 In your English class you have been talking about playing different sports. Now your English teacher has asked you to write an essay for homework.

Write your essay using **all** the notes and giving reasons for your point of view.

Do you think all young people should play a sport?

Notes

Write about:

1. whether it is good for your health
2. what you learn from playing sport
3. .... (your own idea)

Part 2

Write an answer to one of the questions **2–5** in this part. Write your answer in **140–190** words in an appropriate style **on the separate answer sheet**. Put the question number in the box at the top of the answer sheet.

---

2 You have just received this letter from your Canadian friend, Sam.

> As you know, I've just moved to another town and I'm starting at my new school next week. I'm really excited but I don't know anybody yet. What should I do to make friends at school? And how could I meet people near where I live?
>
> Write and tell me what you think.
>
> Sam

Write your **letter**.

3 You recently saw this notice on an international film website for teenagers.

> **Reviews wanted**
>
> **A film all teenagers should see**
>
> Which film would you recommend to young people of your age? Write a review telling us about the story and the main characters, and explain why you think it is a good film for teenagers to see.
>
> The best reviews will be put on our website.

Write your **review**.

4 You have seen this announcement in a new English-language magazine for schools:

> **Stories wanted**
>
> We are looking for stories for our new English-language magazine for teenagers. Your story must begin with this sentence:
>
> *I got to the station and waited nervously for the train to arrive.*
>
> Your story must include:
>
> - a meeting
> - a photograph

Write your **story**.

5 Answer the following question based on the title below.

Macbeth by William Shakespeare

Your English class has had a discussion about the characters in the story of Macbeth. Now your teacher has given you this essay for homework:

Why are the three witches important in the story of Macbeth?

Write your **essay**.

LISTENING (approximately 40 minutes)

Part 1

You will hear people talking in eight different situations. For questions **1–8**, choose the best answer (**A**, **B** or **C**).

---

1 You overhear two friends talking about a lesson they had at school.
What surprised them in the lesson?

A how astronomers are able to research distant stars

B the reason for the particular location of a star

C the temperature and size of the sun

2 You hear two friends talking about buying a card game for the boy's sister.
What is the girl's opinion of it?

A It doesn't suit his sister's character.

B It's not appropriate for someone of his sister's age.

C It's a game that's better for boys than girls.

3 You hear part of an interview on the radio with a writer of children's books.
The writer thinks that books are more powerful than films because

A they affect you in a very personal and vivid way.

B they allow you to share the characters' inner thoughts.

C they stay in your memory longer than films do.

4 You hear a guide speaking to tourists.
What is the guide talking about?

A when different exhibitions are on

B what's on display in the exhibitions

C the best way to go round the exhibitions

5 You hear two friends talking about a musical festival they are going to attend.
What is the boy looking forward to most?

A learning who the surprise performer will be

B having the chance to see new performers

C hearing some performers he liked last year

6 You hear two friends talking about a movie.
What do they agree about?

A The plot was handled appropriately.

B The visual effects were stunning.

C The actors were well chosen.

7 You hear two friends talking about a news story about a baby monkey.
What do they agree about?

A that the monkey is in the best environment for it

B that the monkey deserves better treatment

C that it is sad this species of monkey is endangered

8 You overhear two friends talking about their holidays.
How does the boy feel about his holiday?

A surprised about how much he enjoyed his holiday

B disappointed that the family's plans had to change

C pleased that he was able to learn a new skill

Part 2

You will hear a student called Shirley Bailey giving a talk at her school about her experience of working at a wildlife centre in Africa last summer. For questions **9–18**, complete the sentences with a word or short phrase.

Greenwood Wildlife Centre

When looking for a place to work, Shirley first asked at a

[**9**] near a relative's home.

Shirley explains that Greenwood informs [**10**]

about earning extra income from protecting wildlife.

Shirley found dealing with [**11**]

was the hardest task she had to do at Greenwood.

Shirley was surprised how much she enjoyed doing

[**12**] with certain animals.

Shirley worked on what was called the [**13**] project.

Shirley explains that, generally, animals are put into

[**14**] when they are well enough to leave the zoo.

Shirley found that [**15**]

was her only regular expense after she had arrived at Greenwood.

Shirley says that the best thing about her accommodation was its location near to the

[**16**] .

The centre advised volunteers to wear

[**17**] while they were working.

Greenwood provided the volunteers with [**18**] to use.

Part 3

You will hear five short extracts in which teenagers are talking about the sports they take part in. For questions **19–23**, choose from the list (**A–H**) what each speaker says about their sport. Use the letters only once. There are three extra letters which you do not need to use.

A An injury stopped me doing it for a while.

B I'm going to take a special course to improve my skills.

C I was surprised how much time I needed for it.

D I enjoy competitions more than training.

E It has helped me make a lot of new friends.

F The weather sometimes spoils my enjoyment.

G A member of my family encouraged me to take it up.

H My club provides all the equipment I need.

Speaker 1		**19**
Speaker 2		**20**
Speaker 3		**21**
Speaker 4		**22**
Speaker 5		**23**

Part 4

You will hear part of an interview with Roberto Gianni, a fashion designer. For questions **24–30**, choose the best answer (**A**, **B** or **C**).

---

24 When Roberto was a teenager, he felt he needed

A to show his friends he was capable of originality.

B to prove he was better at design than his friends.

C to help his friends create good-looking clothes.

25 What gave Roberto his big chance to break into the fashion industry?

A going to college to study design

B coming up with an award-winning design

C being interviewed by a fashion magazine

26 How does Roberto feel about the clothes he designs now?

A He thinks they are more glamorous than his early designs.

B He's making clothes that match his own personal taste.

C He believes his designs appeal to different age groups.

27 What does Roberto regard as the biggest influence on his work?

A other more famous designers

B fashion shows he's attended

C the fashions of the past

28 How did Roberto's parents react to his choice of career?

A They gave him their support.

B They tried to change his mind.

C They didn't think he was serious.

29 How does Roberto feel when people are critical of his work?

A He gets upset that they don't understand what he's trying to do.

B He remains confident about what he's doing.

C He is determined to use their feedback constructively.

30 What advice does Roberto have for teenagers who want to become designers?

A find work to gain experience in the business

B study fashion seriously and remain open to new ideas

C create a wide range of designs to show professionals

SPEAKING (14 minutes)

You take the Speaking test with another candidate (possibly two candidates), referred to here as your partner. There are two examiners. One will speak to you and your partner and the other will be listening. Both examiners will award marks.

Part 1 (2 minutes)

The examiner asks you and your partner questions about yourselves. You may be asked about things like 'your home town', 'your interests', 'your career plans', etc.

Part 2 (a one-minute 'long turn' for each candidate, plus a 20-second response from the second candidate)

The examiner gives you two photographs and asks you to talk about them for one minute. The examiner then asks your partner a question about your photographs and your partner responds briefly.

Then the examiner gives your partner two different photographs. Your partner talks about these photographs for one minute. This time the examiner asks you a question about your partner's photographs and you respond briefly.

Part 3 (4 minutes)

The examiner asks you and your partner to talk together. You may be asked to solve a problem or try to come to a decision about something. For example, you might be asked to decide the best way to use some rooms in a language school. The examiner gives you some text to help you but does not join in the conversation.

Part 4 (4 minutes)

The examiner asks some further questions, which leads to a more general discussion of what you have talked about in Part 3. You may comment on your partner's answers if you wish.

Frames for the Speaking test

Test 1

Note: In the examination, there will be both an assessor and an interlocutor in the room.
The visual material for **Test 1** appears on pages C1 and C2 (Part 2), and C3 (Part 3).

Part 1 2 minutes (3 minutes for groups of three)

Interlocutor: Good morning/afternoon/evening. My name is .... and this is my colleague ....
And your names are?
Can I have your mark sheets, please? Thank you.
First of all, we'd like to know something about you.

- Where are you from, *(Candidate A)*?
- And you, *(Candidate B)*?
- What do you like about living *(here / name of candidate's home town)*?
- And what about you, *(Candidate A/B)*?

Select one or more questions from any of the following categories, as appropriate.

Habits and routines
- Do you like to be busy every day? (Why? / Why not?)
- What sport do you enjoy playing? (Why do you like doing that?)
- Do you enjoy watching TV? (What's your favourite programme?) (Why do you like it?)
- Do you ever meet your friends in the evenings after school? (What do you do together?)

The Weekend
- Do you prefer to spend time with your family or with your friends at the weekend? (Why?)
- Are there a lot of interesting things to do in your town at the weekend? (What do you do there?)
- Do you often have to do homework at the weekend? (How do you feel about that?)
- Can you tell us something about what you're planning to do next weekend?

The Future
- What are you going to do after school today? (Why?)
- What would you like to do for your next birthday? (Why?)
- Is there something you'd like to learn in the future? (What would you like to learn?) (Why?)
- What would you like to do when you leave school? (Why?)

Part 2 4 minutes (6 minutes for groups of three)

Family holidays
Celebrations

Interlocutor: In this part of the test, I'm going to give each of you two photographs. I'd like you to talk about your photographs on your own for about a minute, and also to answer a short question about your partner's photographs.

(Candidate A), it's your turn first. Here are your photographs. They show people doing different things on a family holiday.

Indicate pictures 1A and 1B on page C1 to Candidate A.

I'd like you to compare the photographs, and say why you think the people have chosen to do these things on their family holiday. All right?

Candidate A: [*1 minute*]

Interlocutor: Thank you.

(Candidate B), which of these things would you prefer to do with your family? (Why?)

Candidate B: [*Approximately 30 seconds*]

Interlocutor: Thank you.

Now, *(Candidate B)*, here are your photographs. They show people celebrating in different situations.

Indicate pictures 1C and 1D on page C2 to Candidate B.

I'd like you to compare the photographs, and say why you think the people are celebrating in these situations. All right?

Candidate B: [*1 minute*]

Interlocutor: Thank you.

(Candidate A), do you enjoy birthday celebrations? (Why? / Why not?)

Candidate A: [*Approximately 30 seconds*]

Interlocutor: Thank you.

Parts 3 and 4

Part 3 4 minutes (5 minutes for groups of three)

Interlocutor: Now, I'd like you to talk about something together for about two minutes.
[*3 minutes for groups of three*]

I'd like you to imagine that a teacher is planning a class discussion about the place where you live. First you have some time to look at the task.

Indicate the visual 1E on page C3 to the candidates.
Allow 15 seconds.

Now, talk to each other about what the advantages and disadvantages are of having these things near where you live.

Candidates: [*2 minutes / 3 minutes for groups of three*]

Interlocutor: Thank you. Now you have about a minute to decide which of these things it is most important to have near where you live.

Candidates: [*1 minute*]

Interlocutor: Thank you.

Part 4 4 minutes (6 minutes for groups of three)

Interlocutor: *Use the following questions, in order, as appropriate:*

- What's the best thing about living in *(candidate's area)*? (Why?)
- How important is it to live near your friends? (Why?)
- If you could live anywhere in *(candidate's country)*, which town would you choose to live in? (Why?)
- Do you think it might be exciting to live in lots of different places? (Why? / Why not?)
- Some people live in the same place all their lives. What do you think about this?
- Some people go to live and work in other countries. Do you think this is a good thing to do? (Why? / Why not?)

Select any of the following prompts, as appropriate:

- What do you think?
- Do you agree?
- And you?

Thank you. That is the end of the test.

Test 2

Note: In the examination, there will be both an assessor and an interlocutor in the room. The visual material for **Test 2** appears on pages C4 and C5 (Part 2), and C6 (Part 3).

Part 1 2 minutes (3 minutes for groups of three)

Interlocutor: Good morning/afternoon/evening. My name is .... and this is my colleague ....
And your names are?
Can I have your mark sheets, please? Thank you.
First of all, we'd like to know something about you.

- Where are you from, *(Candidate A)*?
- And you, *(Candidate B)*?
- What do you like about living *(here / name of candidate's home town)*?
- And what about you, *(Candidate A/B)*?

Select one or more questions from any of the following categories, as appropriate.

Habits and routines

- Do you like to be busy every day? (Why? / Why not?)
- What sport do you enjoy playing? (Why do you like doing that?)
- Do you enjoy watching TV? (What's your favourite programme?) (Why do you like it?)
- Do you ever meet your friends in the evenings after school? (What do you do together?)

The Weekend

- Do you prefer to spend time with your family or with your friends at the weekend? (Why?)
- Are there a lot of interesting things to do in your town at the weekend? (What do you do there?)
- Do you often have to do homework at the weekend? (How do you feel about that?)
- Can you tell us something about what you're planning to do next weekend?

The Future

- What are you going to do after school today? (Why?)
- What would you like to do for your next birthday? (Why?)
- Is there something you'd like to learn in the future? (What would you like to learn?) (Why?)
- What would you like to do when you leave school? (Why?)

Part 2 4 minutes (6 minutes for groups of three)

Cooking
Taking photos

Interlocutor:	In this part of the test, I'm going to give each of you two photographs. I'd like you to talk about your photographs on your own for about a minute, and also to answer a short question about your partner's photographs.
	(Candidate A), it's your turn first. Here are your photographs. They show people cooking in different situations.
	Indicate pictures 2A and 2B on page C4 to Candidate A.
	I'd like you to compare the photographs, and say why you think the people are cooking in these situations. All right?
Candidate A:	[*1 minute*]
Interlocutor:	Thank you.
	(Candidate B), would you like to cook in either of these situations? (Why? / Why not?)
Candidate B:	[*Approximately 30 seconds*]
Interlocutor:	Thank you.
	Now, *(Candidate B)*, here are your photographs. They show people taking photographs in different situations.
	Indicate pictures 2C and 2D on page C5 to Candidate B.
	I'd like you to compare the photographs, and say why you think the people are taking photographs in these situations. All right?
Candidate B:	[*1 minute*]
Interlocutor:	Thank you.
	(Candidate A), do you like taking photographs when you're on holiday? (Why? / Why not?)
Candidate A:	[*Approximately 30 seconds*]
Interlocutor:	Thank you.

Parts 3 and 4

Part 3 4 minutes (5 minutes for groups of three)

Interlocutor: Now, I'd like you to talk about something together for about two minutes.
[*3 minutes for groups of three*]

Here are some things that many of us try to do in our everyday lives and a question for you to discuss. First you have some time to look at the task.

Indicate the visual 2E on page C6 to the candidates.
Allow 15 seconds.

Now, talk to each other about why it's important to do these things in our everyday lives.

Candidates: [*2 minutes / 3 minutes for groups of three*]

Interlocutor: Thank you. Now you have about a minute to decide which of these things it is most important for everyone to do.

Candidates: [*1 minute*]

Interlocutor: Thank you.

Part 4 4 minutes (6 minutes for groups of three)

Interlocutor: *Use the following questions, in order, as appropriate:*

- What do you enjoy doing most after school each day? (Why?)
- Do you think it's important to eat healthily every day? (Why? / Why not?)
- Do you think life would be better if weekends were longer and everyone had more free time? (Why? / Why not?)
- Some people say that going on the Internet wastes a lot of our time. What do you think?
- Do you think people are happier if they have a very busy life? (Why? / Why not?)
- Some people say you can't have a happy life if you don't work hard. What do you think?
- What do you think is most important for a happy life? (Why? / Why not?)

Select any of the following prompts, as appropriate:

- What do you think?
- Do you agree?
- And you?

Thank you. That is the end of the test.

Test 3

Note: In the examination, there will be both an assessor and an interlocutor in the room. The visual material for **Test 3** appears on pages C7 and C8 (Part 2), and C9 (Part 3).

Part 1 2 minutes (3 minutes for groups of three)

Interlocutor: Good morning/afternoon/evening. My name is .... and this is my colleague ....
And your names are?
Can I have your mark sheets, please? Thank you.
First of all, we'd like to know something about you.

Where are you from, *(Candidate A)*?
And you, *(Candidate B)*?
What do you like about living *(here / name of candidate's home town)*?
And what about you, *(Candidate A/B)*?

Select one or more questions from any of the following categories, as appropriate.

Habits and routines

- Do you like to be busy every day? (Why? / Why not?)
- What sport do you enjoy playing? (Why do you like doing that?)
- Do you enjoy watching TV? (What's your favourite programme?) (Why do you like it?)
- Do you ever meet your friends in the evenings after school? (What do you do together?)

The Weekend

- Do you prefer to spend time with your family or with your friends at the weekend? (Why?)
- Are there a lot of interesting things to do in your town at the weekend? (What do you do there?)
- Do you often have to do homework at the weekend? (How do you feel about that?)
- Can you tell us something about what you're planning to do next weekend?

The Future

- What are you going to do after school today? (Why?)
- What would you like to do for your next birthday? (Why?)
- Is there something you'd like to learn in the future? (What would you like to learn?) (Why?)
- What would you like to do when you leave school? (Why?)

Part 2 4 minutes (6 minutes for groups of three)

Getting help
In town

Interlocutor: In this part of the test, I'm going to give each of you two photographs. I'd like you to talk about your photographs on your own for about a minute, and also to answer a short question about your partner's photographs.

(Candidate A), it's your turn first. Here are your photographs. They show people getting help in different situations.

Indicate pictures 3A and 3B on page C7 to Candidate A.

I'd like you to compare the photographs, and say why you think the people need help in these situations. All right?

Candidate A: [*1 minute*]

Interlocutor: Thank you.

(Candidate B), have you ever needed help with your work? (Why?)

Candidate B: [*Approximately 30 seconds*]

Interlocutor: Thank you.

Now, *(Candidate B)*, here are your photographs. They show people doing different things in town.

Indicate pictures 3C and 3D on page C8 to Candidate B.

I'd like you to compare the photographs, and say why you think the people have chosen to do these things in town. All right?

Candidate B: [*1 minute*]

Interlocutor: Thank you.

(Candidate A), what do you like to do when you're in town? (Why?)

Candidate A: [*Approximately 30 seconds*]

Interlocutor: Thank you.

Parts 3 and 4

Part 3 4 minutes (5 minutes for groups of three)

Interlocutor: Now, I'd like you to talk about something together for about two minutes.
[*3 minutes for groups of three*]

I'd like you to imagine that a teacher is planning a class discussion about what's important for a good education. First you have some time to look at the task.

Indicate the visual 3E on page C9 to the candidates.
Allow 15 seconds.

Now, talk to each other about how important it is for schools to encourage students to do these things as part of their education.

Candidates: [*2 minutes / 3 minutes for groups of three*]

Interlocutor: Thank you. Now you have about a minute to talk about which of these things is not so important for a good education.

Candidates: [*1 minute*]

Interlocutor: Thank you.

Part 4 4 minutes (6 minutes for groups of three)

Interlocutor: *Use the following questions, in order, as appropriate:*

- What do you think is the best thing about your school? (Why?)
- Do you think learning a musical instrument should be part of every student's education? (Why? / Why not?)
- Is it important for all students to do homework? (Why? / Why not?)
- Some schools organise activities for students to do after school or at the weekends. What do you think about this? (Why?)
- Many schools organise trips to other countries for their students. Do you think this is a good idea? (Why? / Why not?)
- What do you think is the right age for students to leave school? (Why?)
- Do you think all students should go to university? (Why? / Why not?)

Select any of the following prompts, as appropriate:

- What do you think?
- Do you agree?
- And you?

Thank you. That is the end of the test.

Test 4

Note: In the examination, there will be both an assessor and an interlocutor in the room.
The visual material for **Test 4** appears on pages C10 and C11 (Part 2), and C12 (Part 3).

Part 1 2 minutes (3 minutes for groups of three)

Interlocutor: Good morning/afternoon/evening. My name is .... and this is my colleague ....
And your names are?
Can I have your mark sheets, please? Thank you.
First of all, we'd like to know something about you.

Where are you from, *(Candidate A)*?
And you, *(Candidate B)*?
What do you like about living *(here / name of candidate's home town)*?
And what about you, *(Candidate A/B)*?

Select one or more questions from any of the following categories, as appropriate.

Habits and routines

- Do you like to be busy every day? (Why? / Why not?)
- What sport do you enjoy playing? (Why do you like doing that?)
- Do you enjoy watching TV? (What's your favourite programme?) (Why do you like it?)
- Do you ever meet your friends in the evenings after school? (What do you do together?)

The Weekend

- Do you prefer to spend time with your family or with your friends at the weekend? (Why?)
- Are there a lot of interesting things to do in your town at the weekend? (What do you do there?)
- Do you often have to do homework at the weekend? (How do you feel about that?)
- Can you tell us something about what you're planning to do next weekend?

The Future

- What are you going to do after school today? (Why?)
- What would you like to do for your next birthday? (Why?)
- Is there something you'd like to learn in the future? (What would you like to learn?) (Why?)
- What would you like to do when you leave school? (Why?)

Part 2 4 minutes (6 minutes for groups of three)

Travelling around a city
A free afternoon

Interlocutor:	In this part of the test, I'm going to give each of you two photographs. I'd like you to talk about your photographs on your own for about a minute, and also to answer a short question about your partner's photographs.
	(Candidate A), it's your turn first. Here are your photographs. They show people travelling around a city in different ways.
	Indicate pictures 4A and 4B on page C10 to Candidate A.
	I'd like you to compare the photographs, and say what you think might be difficult for the people about travelling around a city in these ways. All right?
Candidate A:	[*1 minute*]
Interlocutor:	Thank you.
	(Candidate B), how would you prefer to travel around a city? (Why?)
Candidate B:	[*Approximately 30 seconds*]
Interlocutor:	Thank you.
	Now, *(Candidate B)*, here are your photographs. They show people doing different things on a free afternoon.
	Indicate pictures 4C and 4D on page C11 to Candidate B.
	I'd like you to compare the photographs, and say why you think the people are enjoying doing these things on a free afternoon. All right?
Candidate B:	[*1 minute*]
Interlocutor:	Thank you.
	(Candidate A), which of these things would you prefer to do on a free afternoon? (Why?)
Candidate A:	[*Approximately 30 seconds*]
Interlocutor:	Thank you.

Parts 3 and 4

Part 3 4 minutes (5 minutes for groups of three)

Interlocutor: Now, I'd like you to talk about something together for about two minutes.
[*3 minutes for groups of three*]

Here are some things that might be important if you want to have good friends and a question for you to discuss. First you have some time to look at the task.

Indicate the visual 4E on page C12 to the candidates. Allow 15 seconds.

Now, talk to each other about how important these things are if you want to have good friends.

Candidates: [*2 minutes / 3 minutes for groups of three*]

Interlocutor: Thank you. Now you have about a minute to talk about which two things are most important.

Candidates: [*1 minute*]

Interlocutor: Thank you.

Part 4 4 minutes (6 minutes for groups of three)

Interlocutor: *Use the following questions, in order, as appropriate:*

- How easy do you think it is to make new friends? (Why? / What's the best way to do this?)
- What is the perfect number of friends to have? (Why?)
- How important is it to be able to trust our friends? (Why?)
- What do you think is the main reason why friends argue? (Why?)
- Is it possible to have close friends who are a lot older or younger than us? (Why? / Why not?)
- People in families sometimes find it hard to be friends with each other. Why do you think this is?
- Is it possible to be close friends with people that you only talk to online? (Why? / Why not?)
- Is it easier to be friends with someone who is very similar to you or someone who is very different? (Why?)

Select any of the following prompts, as appropriate:

- What do you think?
- Do you agree?
- And you?

Thank you. That is the end of the test.

Marks and results

Reading and Use of English

Candidates record their answers on a separate answer sheet. Two marks are given for each correct answer in Parts 1 and 2 and one mark is given for each correct answer in Part 3. The total score is then weighted to 40 marks for the whole Reading and Use of English paper.

Writing

Examiners look at four aspects of your writing: Content, Communicative Achievement, Organisation and Language.

Content focuses on how well you have fulfilled the task, in other words if you have done what you were asked to do.

Communicative Achievement focuses on how appropriate the writing is for the letter or story and whether you have used the appropriate register.

Organisation focuses on the way you put the piece of writing together, in other words if it is logical and ordered, and the punctuation is correct.

Language focuses on your vocabulary and grammar. This includes the range of language as well as how accurate it is.

For each of the subscales, the examiner gives a maximum of 5 marks. Examiners use the following assessment scale:

B2	Content	Communicative Achievement	Organisation	Language
5	All content is relevant to the task. Target reader is fully informed.	Uses the conventions of the communicative task effectively to hold the target reader's attention and communicate straightforward and complex ideas, as appropriate.	Text is well-organised and coherent, using a variety of cohesive devices and organisational patterns to generally good effect.	Uses a range of vocabulary, including less common lexis, appropriately. Uses a range of simple and complex grammatical forms with control and flexibility. Occasional errors may be present but do not impede communication.
4	*Performance shares features of Bands 3 and 5.*			
3	Minor irrelevances and/or omissions may be present. Target reader is on the whole informed.	Uses the conventions of the communicative task to hold the target reader's attention and communicate straightforward ideas.	Text is generally well- organised and coherent, using a variety of linking words and cohesive devices.	Uses a range of everyday vocabulary appropriately, with occasional inappropriate use of less common lexis. Uses a range of simple and some complex grammatical forms with a good degree of control. Errors do not impede communication.
2	*Performance shares features of Bands 1 and 3.*			
1	Irrelevances and misinterpretation of task may be present. Target reader is minimally informed.	Uses the conventions of the communicative task in generally appropriate ways to communicate straightforward ideas.	Text is connected and coherent, using basic linking words and a limited number of cohesive devices.	Uses everyday vocabulary generally appropriately, while occasionally overusing certain lexis. Uses simple grammatical forms with a good degree of control. While errors are noticeable, meaning can still be determined.
0	Content is totally irrelevant. Target reader is not informed.	*Performance below Band 1.*		

Length of responses
Make sure you write the correct amount of words. Responses which are too short may not have an adequate range of language and may not provide all the information that is required. Responses which are too long may contain irrelevant content and have a negative effect on the reader.

Varieties of English
You are expected to use a particular variety of English with some degree of consistency in areas such as spelling, and not for example switch from using a British spelling of a word to an American spelling of the same word.

Sample A (Test 1, Question 1 – Essay)

A lot of teenagers spend all their free time on their own, browsing the Internet or playing computer games Of course, this can be both entertaining and educational when used cleverly. Unfortunately, more and more young people spend hours in front of computer screen, isolating themselves from others.

Although I love computer games, I spend most of my free time with my friends. We go cycling, bowling or just walking around in the town. I also go out with my parents from time to time – it really isn't a shame, although some teenagers may think so. I have no idea how I have time for all these things but in the meantime I manage to read tons of books and listen to a lot of music. You can be surprised how much free time you find if you try.

One fantastic idea is to meet with your friends and play volleyball with them for good two hours every weekend. It really gives whole lot of joy and satisfaction.

Scales	Mark	Commentary
Content	5	All the content is relevant and the target reader would be fully informed. The two points in the question are discussed and developed and a third point, the disadvantages of teenagers spending too much time on their own is mentioned.
Communicative Achievement	5	The conventions of essay writing are used effectively to communicate straightforward and some more complex ideas to the reader in an appropriate register, which would hold their attention. The tone is consistent throughout and there is a balanced view taken of the topic.
Organisation	5	The text is well organised and coherent, using a variety of cohesive devices both within and across sentences. The essay makes good use of organisational features such as topic sentences to introduce ideas and comparing and contrasting different opinions.
Language	5	There is a range of topic specific vocabulary used to good effect and there are some nice collocations which are used correctly (*browsing the internet, isolating themselves, walking around*). There is a range of simple and complex grammatical forms used with control and although there are some errors, these do not impede.

Sample B (Test 1, Question 3 – Letter)

Dear Tom,

Thank you for your letter. Sorry that I haven't written for so long. I'd love to advise you what you should choose. Well, to my mind languages play one of the biggest rolw in our modern society. If you want to study abroad or visit foreign country, you ought to speak to pupils by their native language. Moreover, if you are planning to study abroad, you, of course, must know local language.

As for sciences, it also depends on your planning. First of all, you should take shape exactly where you will work. If you decide to connect your future with science, for example physics or chemistry, consequently you should continue studying sciences.

Were I you, I would choose languages, because they become very popular and useful. If you know some language, you could provide your future.

So, your choice depends only on you and your preferences to future. Well, I have to go now. Write back soon and tell me what you choose.

Best wishes,

Ksenia

Scales	Mark	Commentary
Content	5	All content is relevant and the target reader would be fully informed. The writer discusses both languages and sciences and gives an opinion on why each is important, and states which one they would choose.
Communicative Achievement	4	The letter is written in an appropriate, friendly tone, which communicates straightforward ideas effectively. Both advantages and disadvantages of the two subjects are discussed and reasons for choices are given in a way which holds the reader's attention and which would help them make a choice.
Organisation	4	The letter is well organised and coherent and there is a variety of cohesive devices used. The letter has external cohesive features such as *Thank you for your letter*, *Write back soon*, and uses conjunctions to link across and within sentences.
Language	4	There is a range of vocabulary used appropriately with some good phrases attempted; however, less common lexis is not always quite successful (*you should take shape, they become very popular*). There is a range of simple and some more complex grammatical forms used with control. The errors are non-impeding.

Sample C (Test 2, Question 3 – Email)

> *Dear Sarah*
>
> *I am more than happy to help you with your project! In my country, people usually go for their holidays to locations near the place they live in. Whether you live at the east of the country where there are lots of forests and lakes, or at north of the country, near the Baltic sea, there are many places near you that you can visit. Obviously, there are also many things in your city that you do! It doesn't matter if you go swimming in a lake or sea, or if you prefer having a walk in a forest, or simply going to a disco party at the city centre, you can have just as much fun as anywhere else! These are just few activities that young people do in Poland, but probably the most popular ones as well. You can always stay at home, like I usually do. I'm not a great fan of long trips and I find staying at home for holidays and watching TV more enjoyable than anything else. I hope you will find this information useful.*
>
> *Love Peter*

Scales	Mark	Commentary
Content	5	All content is relevant and the target reader would be fully informed. The main topic of holidays is discussed in general terms, describing what young people do in Poland, but there is also the personal aspect at the end.
Communicative Achievement	4	The conventions for informal emails are used effectively here and the target reader's attention would be held. The tone of the email is friendly (*I am more than happy to help*), and informative and it communicates straightforward ideas to the reader.
Organisation	3	The letter is generally well organised and although a variety of linking words and cohesive devices have been used to connect the ideas, paragraphing would help to divide the text more clearly into sections.
Language	4	Everyday vocabulary is used appropriately and there are some very natural phrases (*or simply going, I'm not a great fan of*). There is a range of simple and some more complex grammatical forms used with a good degree of control. Errors mainly occur with prepositions and articles.

Sample D (Test 2, Question 4 – Review)

> *A good café to meet friends in!*
>
> *Here, in Palermo, there are a lot of very beautiful café, but one of the best café to meet friends in is Gino's! It is not in the centre of the centre of the town, it is easy to arrive there by tube, but if you like walking it is only twenty minutes from the principal square.*
>
> *It is the tipical Italian café in a side there is the bar where you can do there breakfast with tea, desserts or croissants, but their specialities are the arancini, you can find more of twenty types of arancini. In the other side there is the restaurant that is also a pizzeria. It serves the best fish of Palermo.*
>
> *There is a very beautiful atmosphere inside very comfortable but at the same time it is funny. I think other people would like it, because in a little space they can find all the Sicily and if the weather is bad it is a very beautiful place where stay with friends.*

Scales	Mark	Commentary
Content	5	All content is relevant to the task and the target reader would be fully informed. We learn where the café is, what food is served and that the atmosphere is good.
Communicative Achievement	4	The conventions of writing a review are used effectively and the target reader's attention would be held. The café is described and both factual and personal observations are made, using a tone and register which are suitable for a teenage audience.
Organisation	2	The review is generally well organised and coherent, making use of linking words and some simple cohesive devices. More use of referencing such as pronouns, rather than punctuation would help the overall cohesiveness of the text, both at sentence and paragraph level.
Language	3	There is a range of everyday vocabulary used appropriately to describe the café. There is a range of simple and some more complex grammatical forms used with a good degree of control. There are some errors, particularly with plurals (*one of the best café*), and prepositions (*more of …; all the Sicily*), but these do not impede communication.

Sample E (Test 3, Question 2 – Article)

What makes a perfect school?

I think that everyone wants to go to school of dreams. It is my wish as well. In next two paragraphs I will tell you what in my opinion makes a perfect school.

Like in any school, teachers should be qualified. They always should behave normally, not to be agressive. What I really don't like is when they aren't in good mood and then they reflect badly on students. I know that they can't always be in good mood, but I don't support their behaviour in these situations because they are nervous and agressive and students usually get bad marks. For me, the perfect teacher is one who is sensitive, who tries to understand us and has positive energy. It's usually smile on his face. How we feel most depends on them.

Second important thing is lesson. They should be normal size. I mean not to be too short or too long. I think that most of students understand lesson much better when it's based on examples. The building of school should be big and spacious classrooms which walls are painted in bright colours. The walls should have some nice flowers. Honestly, what is most important for me is that classes should last 30 minutes, not 45 minutes. This is a 'small picture' of my perfect school.

Scales	Mark	Commentary
Content	4	All the content is relevant and the target reader would be fully informed. Teachers, lessons and the school buildings have been discussed as asked for in the question.
Communicative Achievement	4	The article has been written using the conventions of the article genre in an engaging way. The style and register communicate straightforward ideas effectively for a teenage audience, using personal examples to support opinions, which would hold the attention of the reader.
Organisation	3	The text is generally well organised and coherent. There is a variety of linking words and cohesive devices, but there is some repetition of key points which could be avoided if more referencing words were used and if the paragraphs were developed more cohesively.
Language	4	There is a range of vocabulary attempted (*positive energy, based on examples, spacious*) but when more abstract or more complex ideas are expressed, it is not always successful (*a school of dreams, they reflect badly on*). There is a range of simple and complex grammatical forms used with control, and although there are errors, these do not impede.

Sample F (Test 3, Question 4 – Story)

A tropical experience

Robert was excited as he jumped into the boat. It all began when he arrived on the island.

The clear water was warm and full of playful and colourful fish. The island was covered by hug palmtrees which were blocking the light from the sun to enter the tropical forest. Robert entered the forest amazed by the creatures that were living on the island. As he was walking, he saw a huge cave surrounded by tropical plants. He entered the cave. It was dark inside, so he knew that there were bats. He walked quietly around a lake. The blue water was catching small sun beams. As he was leaning towards the water he heard a loud noise. A big group of bats was heading towards him. He started to run as fast as he could.

As he was aproaching his boat, he saw a gold ring. He took the ring and put it in his pocket. A thought of his fiancé came in his mind.

Robert jumped in his boat and went home thinking of all the experiences he went through that day.

Scales	Mark	Commentary
Content	5	All the content is relevant and the target reader would be on the whole informed due to the story not following on from the prompt completely logically. There is not a clear connection between the first two sentences.
Communicative Achievement	4	The story uses some of the features of a narrative effectively to communicate straightforward ideas, there is description and the scene setting is clear. There is a range of narrative tenses, particularly in the second paragraph where the story develops well and the target reader's attention would be held.
Organisation	3	The text is generally well organised, more linking between separate events would make the connections clearer to the reader. The text is coherent and there is some good use of sequential cohesive devices which progress the story.
Language	4	There is a good range of vocabulary which is used appropriately to set the scene and describe the island. There is a range of simple and some more complex grammatical forms, and although there are some errors with tenses these do not impede communication.

Sample G (Test 4, Question 1 – Essay)

People have played sport for ages. In ancient Greece there were Olympic Games The winner has amazing glory and his name was well known in the whole country. It have to mean something so I think everyone should play a sport. It don't have to be professional sport. It could be even jogging in the park.

Many scientists, medicine doctors, etc. say that sport improve our phisical condition and make us happy. Some people feel relaxed when they are training after really stressful day. People who play a sport have illness less often than those who sit in front of television or computer. It's a fact. Bones of people who train are stronger, their muscles are more powerful and they look better than the others.

I play football, volleyball and handball. This game teach me how to cooperate with my teammates. I do karate also. It makes me relaxed even when I'm exhausted after training. You never know what happens and you have to focus on your task. It helps me in my normal life.

People should play a sport just for their own good.

Scales	Mark	Commentary
Content	5	All the content is relevant and the target reader would be fully informed. The two points in the question are developed appropriately and a third aspect, the glory of winning and being successful, is touched on.
Communicative Achievement	4	The essay uses the conventions of the communicative task effectively to present and develop the ideas in a way which holds the target reader's attention. Straightforward ideas are presented in a neutral tone and world knowledge is used to support opinions, for example the Olympic Games in Greece.
Organisation	3	The essay is generally well organised and coherent. Some of the shorter sentences could be joined to make more compound sentences, but there is a variety of linking words and cohesive devices, such as relative clauses and referencing pronouns which are used appropriately throughout the text.
Language	3	There is a range of everyday vocabulary used appropriately, and there are some nice phrases (*jogging in the park, cooperate with my teammates*). There is a range of simple and some more complex grammatical forms used with a good degree of control. The repeated errors (*sport improve, This game teach me*) do not impede.

Sample H (Test 4, Question 3 – Review)

There is an exciting book under the title "The Lost World", written by A Conan Doyle, which was made into a film and recently I've watched it. I would recommend it to young people of my age, because I find it really interesting.

The plot revolves around the adventures of Mr Challenger and his followers. The professor is the main character of the story, he's so devoted to his ideas! Another personality is a journalist, Mr Mallow, who is also fascinating. At the beginning of the film Mr Challenger tells that he sees some photos of unusual lands and plants and decides to find them. Later, the group find the place, where there are prehistoric people and animals. They return home and by the end of the story everyone has to believe them, because they show one of the creatures.

I was deeply impressed by the film and believe that teenagers will be interested in it as it stirs our imagination. Besides, it's fast-moving and what is more it has some twists. To my mind, it's really worth watching.

Scales	Mark	Commentary
Content	5	All the content is relevant and the target reader would be fully informed. The review describes the plot, the characters and makes a recommendation.
Communicative Achievement	4	The conventions of writing a review are used effectively to hold the target reader's attention. There is good use of adjectives when describing the film and both factual, objective observations and personal opinions are offered in a positive tone, which is engaging.
Organisation	5	The text is well organised and coherent using a range of cohesive devices to good effect. The overall structure of the review is well planned, describing the origins of the film, the events in the film and finally offering a recommendation.
Language	5	There is a range of vocabulary which is used appropriately, including good use of adjectives and some interesting verbs (*the plot revolves, so devoted to, deeply impressed, stirs our imagination*). Good control is shown over a range of grammatical forms and although there are a few errors, these are minimal and do not impede.

Listening

One mark is given for each correct answer. The total is weighted to give a mark out of 40 for the paper. In Part 2, minor spelling errors are allowed, provided that the candidate's intention is clear.

For security reasons, several versions of the Listening paper are used at each administration of the examination. Before grading, the performance of the candidates in each of the versions is compared and marks adjusted to compensate for any imbalance in levels of difficulty.

Speaking

Throughout the test candidates are assessed on their own individual performance and not in relation to the other candidate. They are assessed on their language skills, not on their personality, intelligence or knowledge of the world. Candidates must, however, be prepared to develop the conversation and respond to the tasks in an appropriate way.

Candidates are awarded marks by two examiners: the assessor and the interlocutor. The assessor awards marks by applying performance descriptors from the Analytical Assessment scales for the following criteria:

Grammar and Vocabulary

This refers to the accurate use of grammatical forms and appropriate use of vocabulary. It also includes the range of language.

Discourse Management

This refers to the extent, relevance and coherence of each candidate's contributions. Candidates should be able to construct clear stretches of speech which are easy to follow. The length of their contributions should be appropriate to the task, and what they say should be related to the topic and the conversation in general.

Pronunciation

This refers to the intelligibility of contributions at word and sentence levels. Candidates should be able to produce utterances that can easily be understood, and which show control of intonation, stress and individual sounds.

Interactive Communication

This refers to the ability to use language to achieve meaningful communication. Candidates should be able to initiate and respond appropriately according to the task and conversation, and also to use interactive strategies to maintain and develop the communication whilst negotiating towards an outcome.

B2	Grammar and Vocabulary	Discourse Management	Pronunciation	Interactive Communication
5	• Shows a good degree of control of a range of simple and some complex grammatical forms. • Uses a range of appropriate vocabulary to give and exchange views on a wide range of familiar topics.	• Produces extended stretches of language with very little hesitation. • Contributions are relevant and there is a clear organisation of ideas. • Uses a range of cohesive devices and discourse markers.	• Is intelligible. • Intonation is appropriate. • Sentence and word stress is accurately placed. • Individual sounds are articulated clearly.	• Initiates and responds appropriately, linking contributions to those of other speakers. • Maintains and develops the interaction and negotiates towards an outcome.
4	*Performance shares features of Bands 3 and 5.*			
3	• Shows a good degree of control of simple grammatical forms, and attempts some complex grammatical forms. • Uses a range of appropriate vocabulary to give and exchange views on a range of familiar topics.	• Produces extended stretches of language despite some hesitation. • Contributions are relevant and there is very little repetition. • Uses a range of cohesive devices.	• Is intelligible. • Intonation is generally appropriate. • Sentence and word stress is generally accurately placed. • Individual sounds are generally articulated clearly.	• Initiates and responds appropriately. • Maintains and develops the interaction and negotiates towards an outcome with very little support.
2	*Performance shares features of Bands 1 and 3.*			
1	• Shows a good degree of control of simple grammatical forms. • Uses a range of appropriate vocabulary when talking about everyday situations.	• Produces responses which are extended beyond short phrases, despite hesitation. • Contributions are mostly relevant, despite some repetition. • Uses basic cohesive devices.	• Is mostly intelligible, and has some control of phonological features at both utterance and word levels.	• Initiates and responds appropriately. • Keeps the interaction going with very little prompting and support.
0	*Performance below Band 1.*			

The interlocutor awards a mark for overall performance using a Global Achievement scale.

B2	Grammar and Vocabulary
5	• Handles communication on a range of familiar topics, with very little hesitation. • Uses accurate and appropriate linguistic resources to express ideas and produce extended discourse that is generally coherent.
4	*Performance shares features of Bands 3 and 5.*
3	• Handles communication on familiar topics, despite some hesitation. • Organises extended discourse but occasionally produces utterances that lack coherence, and some inaccuracies and inappropriate usage occur.
2	*Performance shares features of Bands 1 and 3.*
1	• Handles communication in everyday situations, despite hesitation. • Constructs longer utterances but is not able to use complex language except in well-rehearsed utterances.
0	*Performance below Band 1.*

Assessment for *Cambridge English: First for Schools* is based on performance across all parts of the test, and is achieved by applying the relevant descriptors in the assessment scales.

Test 1 Key

Reading and Use of English (1 hour 15 minutes)

Part 1

1 D **2** A **3** C **4** B **5** D **6** B **7** C **8** B

Part 2

9 had / held **10** Although / Though **11** other **12** and **13** what
14 That / This **15** one / some **16** be / come

Part 3

17 growth **18** scientists **19** behaviour / behavior **20** equipment
21 recording(s) **22** discovery **23** unaware **24** valuable / invaluable / valued

Part 4

25 GET the brakes | checked OR GET a | brake check
26 lent me | her car UNTIL
27 would have / would've / 'd have been / arrived | on / in TIME
28 from Nicky | NOBODY has put / written OR from Nicky | NOBODY (else) put / wrote
29 WISH I had / 'd / paid (more) OR WISH I had / 'd | been paying
30 've / have RUN out | of

Part 5

31 D **32** C **33** B **34** A **35** A **36** C

Part 6

37 D **38** A **39** E **40** G **41** F **42** C

Part 7

43 D **44** C **45** A **46** C **47** B **48** A **49** B **50** D **51** C **52** B

Writing (1 hour 20 minutes)

Candidate responses are marked using the assessment scale on page 108.

Listening (approximately 40 minutes)

Part 1

1 C 2 B 3 A 4 A 5 C 6 C 7 B 8 A

Part 2

9 film / movie **10** (tour) guide **11** mountain / Mountain
12 jungle(-)life / junglelife **13** peaceful **14** insects
15 black(-)back(s) / blackback(s) **16** ground
17 humans / human beings **18** rainforest / Rainforest

Part 3

19 D 20 B 21 H 22 F 23 E

Part 4

24 C 25 A 26 B 27 B 28 C 29 A 30 A

Transcript

This is the Cambridge English: First for Schools, Test 1.

I'm going to give you the instructions for this test. I'll introduce each part of the test and give you time to look at the questions. At the start of each piece you'll hear this sound:

tone

You'll hear each piece twice.

Remember, while you're listening, write your answers on the question paper. You'll have five minutes at the end of the test to copy your answers onto the separate answer sheet.

There will now be a pause. Please ask any questions now, because you must not speak during the test.

[pause]

Now open your question paper and look at Part One.

[pause]

PART 1 *You'll hear people talking in eight different situations. For questions 1–8, choose the best answer (A, B or C).*

Question 1 *One. You hear part of a news item about a school project.*

[pause]

tone

Man: Students at the Central School in Newtown have won a national competition to find the best eco-invention. Competitors had to find a way to change a familiar place, making it better for the environment. The winners came up with an idea they called the Centi-Pedal to be used by people waiting in a queue for ice cream in a local park. Their invention is a long stationary bike with eight seats. Kids waiting in line take turns to pedal. This makes the wait less boring and also helps to power the ice cream freezers. Anyone pedalling for more than five minutes gets a discount on their ice cream.

[pause]

tone

[The recording is repeated.]

[pause]

Question 2 *Two. You hear a teacher talking to her students about a writing competition.*

[pause]

tone

Woman: I know you're all very interested in the short story competition so I'm very glad to tell you that you're all registered and your contributions have to be handed in by the end of the month – so there isn't much time to get the revised final versions done. I'm going to give you back your first drafts with some individual comments. Your work shows plenty of imagination, which is a definite plus, but a general point to bear in mind is that stories which have been successful in this competition in previous years have tended to follow a traditional structure with a beginning, middle and end, even though they were only three or four pages long.

[pause]

tone

[The recording is repeated.]

[pause]

Question 3 *Three. You hear part of a radio item about a bird.*

[pause]

tone

Woman: A rare white kiwi bird has been born in New Zealand as part of a special breeding programme. The bird, named Manukura by members of the local Maori community, was born at the Pukaha Mount Bruce National Wildlife Centre and is believed to be the first all-white kiwi chick ever to have been born in captivity. The arrival of the bird was a big surprise as no white kiwis had been brought to the Wildlife Centre. It is believed that Manukura's parents must have carried the genes for white feathers. Local Maoris have called the bird's birth a 'tohu' which means a sign of new beginnings.

[pause]

tone

[The recording is repeated.]

[pause]

Question 4 *Four. You hear two friends talking about a TV talent show.*

[pause]

tone

Girl: What did you think of last night's 'Pop Stars' programme?

Boy: Well, some of the competitors were really good this week.

Girl: Do you think so? I did like the guy who sang last. I thought he had a very powerful voice.

Boy: Really? I thought he was a bit boring. I preferred the group of girls who opened the show.

Girl: Well, they looked good but wasn't it a strange song for them to pick?

Boy: You can say that again! But they did it very well.

Girl: Hmm. But I'm really not getting into it. I hope things improve next week.

Boy: I'm sure they will.

[pause]

tone

[The recording is repeated.]

[pause]

Question 5 *Five. You hear a girl talking about a sports event she took part in.*

[pause]

tone

Girl: I recently won a trophy at a big football club. I raised money for a children's charity by asking friends and family to sponsor me in a running race. It was quite cold on the day but, before we started, we had a dancing warm-up with music, to get us ready. We ran two laps around the outside of the stadium. There were lots of really kind, supportive people cheering us all the way round, which was fun. At the end it got hard but I managed to keep going. Then a man handed me a medal and said I was the first girl to finish. I was surprised as I hadn't expected that.

[pause]

tone

[The recording is repeated.]

[pause]

Question 6 *Six. You hear a teacher telling her class about something called World Oceans Day.*

[pause]

tone

Woman: Now, next week there's going to be a special international day called World Oceans Day. The organisers want everyone all over the world to think about protecting our oceans, which generate the oxygen we breathe, help feed us, regulate our climate, and clean the water we drink, as well as being home to hundreds of species of underwater creatures. So what do you think we could do to make our commitment to protect the oceans on that day? In a moment, I'm going to give you a few ideas about that. Then you can come up with some ideas of your own for homework and we'll make our decision.

[pause]

tone

[The recording is repeated.]

[pause]

Question 7 *Seven. You hear an announcement about a festival.*

[pause]

tone

Man: How do you fancy winning the chance to take your family to a fantastic music festival over the midsummer weekend? Happy Times Music Festival is now in its second year and it looks set to give all those attending a wonderful weekend. The Festival focuses on the best music of the last fifty years with top artists performing hits from the past as well as those of today. To win a family ticket send us a text saying, in no more than fifteen words, why you'd like to be there. Tickets are selling fast so this might be your only chance to get there.

[pause]

tone

[The recording is repeated.]

[pause]

Question 8 *Eight. You hear a boy leaving a voicemail message for his friend.*

[pause]

tone

Boy: Hi, Gary. I got your message. The funny thing is my mum's just like yours. She's always asking me what I think she should get my cousins for their birthdays. I don't know why she thinks I'm such a good person to ask. Anyway, about that computer game you asked me about – *All Stars Racing*. Well, I've heard of it but I've never played it so I've got no idea if it'd be good for your cousin. I don't mind going with you to that games place in the shopping centre to try it out if you think that'd help. All right. Text me if you like. Bye.

[pause]

tone

[The recording is repeated.]

[pause]

That is the end of Part One.

Now turn to Part Two.

[pause]

PART 2

You'll hear a boy called Joe giving a class presentation about a project he's done on the subject of gorillas. For questions 9–18, complete the sentences with a word or short phrase.

You now have forty-five seconds to look at Part Two.

[pause]

tone

Joe: Hi. Today I'm going to tell you about the project I've done all about gorillas, an animal that's interested me ever since I was little. I remember being given an amazing book about them with loads of wonderful pictures in it. That was because I'd watched a film about them when I was about seven and they'd really captured my imagination. Unfortunately, I couldn't find that book when I was doing my project, which was a shame.

My uncle also helped keep my enthusiasm going. He's a teacher now, but for a time he had a job as a tour guide in the south-west of Uganda, which is one of the gorilla's main habitats – they can also be found in Rwanda and the Democratic Republic of Congo. He's a keen photographer in his spare time and he sent me lots of photos he took while he was there.

It's generally agreed that there are several types of gorilla: Lowland gorillas, Cross River gorillas and also Mountain gorillas, which were the ones my uncle saw and took pictures of. These names obviously reflect the environments they're typically found in.

I'll show you some of his pictures later on but the majority of the ones I've got for you – as well as the stuff I'm going to tell you about – come from a website called jungle-life.com. I also used another website called animal-ways.com. Although it was less useful for this project, it did have some interesting stuff about conservation work being done to help protect gorillas.

People often think of gorillas as large aggressive animals, thumping their chests and making scary noises. But I discovered from my research that they're not actually fierce at all. They're peaceful unless they're threatened in some way.

Gorillas are mainly herbivores, which means that although they are very large creatures, they manage on a diet of plants. They eat all sorts of shoots and leaves, for example. They can occasionally also be seen eating insects, apparently, which I hadn't realised. And despite the fact that they live in a very hot climate, these animals are very rarely observed drinking – they seem to get enough water from their diet, without needing anything extra.

A group of Mountain gorillas usually consists of one or two younger males, a few females and their young. This group is lead by the dominant male, who's known as the silverback. It's a good name because it refers to the way the adult male's coat turns from black to grey as he matures. And you won't be surprised to hear that the blackback is the name given to the less mature male gorillas.

Like other apes, gorillas build nests. Many apes, for example chimpanzees, make their nests in trees, whereas gorillas make theirs on the ground, pulling down branches to do this. The young share a nest with their mothers but once they're about three years old they move into their own.
Gorillas don't have many predators. The main animals that are a threat to them are leopards, wild cats and of course other larger gorillas. However, sadly, humans are their greatest enemy and that's the same story with many endangered animals today.

If you'd like to find out more about these wonderful animals, there are a number of good books about gorillas in the school library. I'd suggest you read this book by Carola Newcombe. It's called *Gorillas in the Rainforest*. There's another book by Thomas Pane called *Gorillas in the Wild*. I don't think that's quite so interesting in fact, but both these books are better than *Gorillas in Danger*, which is a bit depressing.

Anyway, I'd like to show you some of the photos I ...

[pause]

Now you'll hear Part Two again.

tone

[The recording is repeated.]

[pause]

That is the end of Part Two.

Now turn to Part Three.

[pause]

PART 3

You'll hear five short extracts in which teenagers are talking about a recent holiday. For questions 19–23, choose from the list (A–H) the opinion each speaker expresses. Use the letters only once. There are three extra letters which you do not need to use.

You now have thirty seconds to look at Part Three.

[pause]

tone

Speaker 1

[pause]

I had a brilliant holiday in Greece this summer. My best friend's parents invited me to go with them to visit their cousins. It was great 'cause they speak Greek and know where to go and what to do. We saw fantastic archaeological sites and also went scuba diving several times. I loved that – and felt I'd really improved since my first attempts last year. Probably the best thing was going to an opera in an ancient open-air theatre. I wasn't looking forward to it because I'd never seen an opera before, but I can't wait to go again!

[pause]

Speaker 2

[pause]

This year my family went to France. I've been learning French at school but I didn't get to practise it much because everyone there spoke English much better than I spoke French. We stayed in a campsite on the south coast. It was a terribly long drive down there, which was boring, but it was fun once we arrived. There were loads of people my age staying there too and we spent every day together. Some of us had waterskiing lessons. I've always wanted to have a go at that and it turned out I had a real talent for it. I hope I'll persuade my parents to go back there next year.

[pause]

Speaker 3

[pause]

We usually go to the same place every year. You might think that's a bit boring but I actually like it. I've got some of my best friends there – we've all known each other since we were six. This year we took some cousins along with us. They're from Australia and they're spending a year travelling round the world. Lucky things! I'd never met them before. It was fun being on holiday with them, showing them round and introducing them to my mates. They particularly enjoyed some evenings we spent at a jazz club. I did too – the musicians were great, and it's made me determined to start learning the saxophone now I'm home.

[pause]

Speaker 4

[pause]

This year we went to Spain for the first time. It was exciting because my brother and I did loads of surfing. Neither of us had ever even been on a surf board before. My brother seemed to get the hang of it at once. I never did, but I still enjoyed it. What was great, though, was that I'm the only person in my family who knows any Spanish so I did all the ordering in restaurants. It was kind of fun being in charge of things actually! The journey home was exciting – we missed our flight and ended up coming home by train!

[pause]

Speaker 5

[pause]

I went away with my grandma this year. I'd only ever been away with her on my own once before and that was ages ago. So I was a bit apprehensive, you know, thinking she might want to do very different things from me. But it was fine. We both love music so most evenings we ate in a café, where people used to come to play folk music. But the highlight for me was actually getting there. We drove to the cottage she'd rented and it took us four or five days. Not because it was that far, but because we stopped to do lots of things along the way.

[pause]

Now you'll hear Part Three again.

tone

[The recording is repeated.]

[pause]

That is the end of Part Three.

Now turn to Part Four.

[pause]

PART 4

You'll hear an interview with a writer called Clare Watson, who writes novels for teenagers. For questions 24–30, choose the best answer (A, B or C).

You now have one minute to look at Part Four.

[pause]

tone

Interviewer: With me in the studio today, I have Clare Watson, author of over twenty extremely successful novels for teenagers. Clare, what first made you want to become a novelist?

Clare: I've always loved books. I can remember as a very small child listening to my mum reading stories to me. At primary school, we'd write stories and the teacher often chose me to read mine aloud to the rest of the class. However, at secondary school, the teacher was more interested in perfect spelling and grammar so I started getting lots of corrections and lost some of my enthusiasm. But I still used to make up stuff to entertain my kid brother. He said my stories were way better than anything in books. That's what started me thinking maybe I could write one for publication one day.

Interviewer: You've published lots of novels. Do you have a personal favourite?

Clare: It's hard to decide, I think it's probably *Swans*. It's one of my funniest stories, but that's not why I like it so much. It's more because it ended up just how I'd imagined it being. Each time I start a novel, I want it to be this and that and it hardly ever becomes what I'd intended. Anyway, it's about Gina Finlay, the girl I've written twelve other novels about, but it's the first one set in a holiday context. The previous ones had all been about Gina at school.

Interviewer: How do you come up with ideas for stories?

Clare: Well, that's a bit like asking where you get your dreams from. You don't exactly know, do you? Dreams are often quite surprising and you've no idea really where they originate. But I came up with my first idea for the Gina Finlay series when I was jogging round the park. In fact, that's where most of my ideas make their first appearance.

Interviewer: The Gina Finlay stories have become a phenomenally successful TV series. How do you feel about the TV adaptations?

Clare: I'm glad Gina's become so popular. For years, I'd been getting letters from fans saying, please get her stories made into TV shows. When that eventually happened, I don't think anyone imagined it'd turn into such a long-running series. I enjoy visiting the set and watching the actors at work, but I don't have to write the scripts, thank goodness! There are so many that it wouldn't be possible. But the team of writers does a great job, I think!

Interviewer: You've set up a project to encourage teenagers to write fiction. What was the inspiration for that?

Clare: Yes, I work with teenagers, setting up writing groups at schools all over the country. It's so rewarding. Most days now I get letters from kids telling me how they're getting on. The idea came to me when a friend told me about a successful writing group which had been set up in an Australian school. I talked about it with some fellow authors and we all felt it could work here too.

Interviewer: How did you feel when you won that big award last year?

Clare: When I knew I'd been short-listed, I couldn't believe it and I was thrilled when I won because there are lots of excellent novels for teenagers around these days. I take it very seriously because I'm following in some remarkable footsteps, like Mary Green, the author I admire above all others; she got it a few years ago. I realised it'd involve new responsibilities, but I'm always excited by new challenges so I don't mind that.

Interviewer: How do you manage to write about teens' emotions so well?

Clare: Well, I taught teenagers for a few years after graduating and that might've helped a little. Especially as not many of my own kids or nephews and nieces have reached their teens yet. I think the main thing, though, is that I still recall very vividly my own feelings as a teenager. It's a long time ago but it doesn't seem that way somehow.

Interviewer: Thanks very much, Clare.

[pause]

Now you'll hear Part Four again.

tone

[The recording is repeated.]

[pause]

That is the end of Part Four.

There will now be a pause of five minutes for you to copy your answers onto the separate answer sheet. Be sure to follow the numbering of all the questions. I'll remind you when there's one minute left so that you're sure to finish in time.

[Teacher, pause the recording here for five minutes. Remind your students when they have one minute left.]

That's the end of the test. Please stop now. Your supervisor will now collect all the question papers and answer sheets.

Test 2 Key

Reading and Use of English (1 hour 15 minutes)

Part 1

1 B **2** A **3** D **4** B **5** D **6** C **7** B **8** C

Part 2

9 to **10** known **11** from **12** what **13** it **14** their **15** which
16 coming

Part 3

17 understanding **18** individually **19** instructions **20** unclear **21** enjoyable
22 educational / educative **23** locations **24** availability

Part 4

25 not INTERESTED in | being / becoming
26 WOULD have / WOULD've gone / been skating | if
27 haven't / have not / 've not SEEN | David for / in
28 this computer | is DIFFERENT
29 in SPITE of | (the) wind
30 time | I GOT to the

Part 5

31 A **32** C **33** B **34** D **35** C **36** B

Part 6

37 E **38** D **39** G **40** A **41** F **42** B

Part 7

43 B **44** A **45** C **46** A **47** D **48** B **49** A **50** D
51 C **52** D

Writing (1 hour 20 minutes)

Candidate responses are marked using the assessment scale on page 108.

Listening (approximately 40 minutes)

Part 1

1 C **2** B **3** A **4** A **5** B **6** B **7** C **8** C

Part 2

9 honey **10** gardens **11** gold **12** tomato **13** saucer **14** steam (power)
15 (chocolate) press **16** bars **17** milk **18** mood(s)

Part 3

19 B **20** C **21** F **22** D **23** G

Part 4

24 A **25** C **26** B **27** A **28** C **29** B **30** C

Transcript

This is the Cambridge English: First for Schools, Test 2.

I'm going to give you the instructions for this test. I'll introduce each part of the test and give you time to look at the questions. At the start of each piece you'll hear this sound.

tone

You'll hear each piece twice.

Remember, while you're listening, write your answers on the question paper. You'll have five minutes at the end of the test to copy your answers onto the separate answer sheet.

There will now be a pause. Please ask any questions now, because you must not speak during the test.

[pause]

Now open your question paper and look at Part One.

[pause]

PART 1 *You'll hear people talking in eight different situations. For questions 1–8, choose the best answer (A, B or C).*

Question 1 *One. You hear a teacher talking to some students.*

[pause]

tone

Man: Now I took this photo when I was on holiday by the sea. I was walking along a path on the southern coast. To get across the river that runs into this shallow bay here, I had to head away from the seashore. And I was struck by the change in character of the soil and what was growing as I got further away from the shore. There was a real contrast between the thin soil on top of the cliffs there, and the grass and plants that you can see in the picture as I got further inland. Look at the thick woods and green fields here.

[pause]

tone

[The recording is repeated.]

[pause]

Question 2 *Two. You hear two friends talking about a bike race they went on.*

[pause]

tone

Boy: Are you pleased you did the bike race?

Girl: Well, forty kilometres is a long way to cycle. I was exhausted by the end so I think doing that distance in the time I did it was quite an achievement, even if it was slow compared to some of the others. But, you know, in the last ten kilometres my legs were feeling really sore. I didn't realise just how hard that'd make it, but I kept going, and I can't say I ever really thought about giving up. I guess we were lucky to get so much encouragement from people watching.

Boy: It made quite a difference, didn't it?

[pause]

tone

[The recording is repeated.]

[pause]

Question 3 *Three. You hear a man and his daughter talking in a library.*

[pause]

tone

Girl: I don't know what book to take out this week, Dad. Have you got any ideas?

Man: Well, you used to like stories by Jackie Donald. Perhaps they've got one of hers that you haven't read yet?

Girl: Oh, I'm not so keen on her now – I need a change.

Man: Well, whatever you choose, please hurry up because we haven't got all day. What about that biography of the dancer you like. Shall I find it for you? But, look, I did promise Mum we'd be home by six.

Girl: Well, I do like stories about people's lives, I suppose.

[pause]

tone

[The recording is repeated.]

[pause]

Question 4 *Four. You hear two friends talking about a television programme about polar bears.*

[pause]

tone

Boy: Did you watch the documentary about those polar bears stuck on an iceberg for weeks?

Girl: Yeah, I loved it! I've seen lots of programmes about polar bears but this one seemed quite different.

Boy: The close-ups of the bears were amazing but you get that kind of thing in most wildlife programmes, don't you?

Girl: True. But the scenery was fantastic – I suppose it's not hard to make icebergs look impressive, though. But you'd never believe the stuff about why the bears stayed on that iceberg.

Boy: You mean because they were scared to leave? I'd never heard of anything like that before either. You wouldn't think they'd be afraid of anything.

[pause]

tone

[The recording is repeated.]

[pause]

Question 5 *Five. You hear a teacher talking to a class.*

[pause]

tone

Woman: OK, class. I'm going to ask you to do something rather different today. As you know, the school's holding an open day for families and friends in two weeks' time and we're going to be selling various things to make some money for a children's charity. Our class is going to make some small cakes to sell on the day. Next week, I'll ask you to bring in different ingredients from home and then we'll make the cakes here in school. But tonight I want you to ask all your friends and relations what their favourite kind of cake is. That'll help us decide exactly what cakes we're going to make.

[pause]

tone

[The recording is repeated.]

[pause]

Question 6 *Six. You hear two friends talking about a story-writing competition.*

[pause]

tone

Boy: Are you going to enter that competition our teacher told us about? I think you should. You're great at writing short stories.

Girl: Thanks, but you have to write about a wild animal. I don't know much about animals and haven't a clue what I could write about.

Boy: I could help you. You could make up a great story about an elephant, for example. I did a project on them last year and could give you some background information. I'd want to have part of the prize, of course!

Girl: Well, it's a trip to London Zoo for four so you could come with me and my parents.

Boy: Great! Let's get started!

[pause]

tone

[The recording is repeated.]

[pause]

Question 7 *Seven. You hear a radio announcement about an event.*

[pause]

tone

Woman: Scientists studying wildlife are keen to find out more about the creatures that you generally find living in city gardens and are asking for your help. If you see or hear any birds or animals in your backyard, please get in touch. Last year over a hundred thousand people took part in our similar survey and it's hoped even more will participate this time. The survey's important because it helps us know which types of creature are doing well and which are in decline.
If you're willing to get involved, then log on to the Nature Count website at www.naturecount.com. We'll give the address again later in the programme.

[pause]

tone

[The recording is repeated.]

[pause]

Question 8 *Eight. You hear a review of a computer game on the radio.*

[pause]

tone

Man: A game that's been popular for some time in the US has just had its first release here. *Alien Attack* starts you off protecting a small mountain village from attack by aliens but you soon find you're actually living in a dream world. Your adventures then start to cross over from one world to the other as your actions in one affect what happens in the other. It can be tricky to figure out what on earth's going on at some points but, if you're a fan of adventure games, you'll probably love this one. It's not a good choice for people new to games like this, however.

[pause]

tone

[The recording is repeated.]

[pause]

That is the end of Part One.

Now turn to Part Two.

[pause]

PART 2

You'll hear a girl called Kate giving a class presentation on the subject of chocolate. For questions 9–18, complete the sentences with a word or short phrase.

You now have forty-five seconds to look at Part Two.

[pause]

tone

Kate: My presentation today is about chocolate. When our teacher said we could do a history project on any food we liked, I knew straight away what I'd choose, because chocolate's my absolute favourite.

So where does the story of chocolate begin? More than fifteen hundred years ago, seed pods from the cocoa tree were being used to make chocolate by people in Central America. I discovered that the Mayan civilization in Mexico were the first people to realise that cocoa beans are absolutely delicious. They made a chocolate drink, which was sweetened with honey, but which, incredibly, also contained chilli peppers – can you imagine that?

To begin with, the cocoa pods were collected from wild trees in the rainforest, but soon chocolate became so popular that people started cultivating them. This was in gardens, however, rather than in fields on farms. This, of course, made it much easier for people to get hold of chocolate and its consumption became widespread.

Another civilization, the Aztecs, learnt from their Mayan neighbours how delicious chocolate was as a drink and they eventually valued it so highly that the beans were accepted as a way of paying taxes, even though gold was widely available.

Cocoa didn't make its way to Europe until the fifteenth century. Spanish explorers in the Americas took it home with them along with the potato, but it is thought that the tomato was taken over to Europe even earlier than this.

Chocolate became fashionable in Europe in the seventeenth century and people used to meet in chocolate houses to chat and drink chocolate – a bit like the way people meet in cafés today. They drank their chocolate from a special dish with two handles and it was because of this that the saucer first made its appearance – it kept the chocolate from dripping onto people's clothes.

In seventeen ninety-five, J. Fry and Sons, an English company, started to use steam power to grind cocoa beans by machine for the first time. This was a great step forward as up until then, cocoa beans had been ground by hand on hard surfaces such as stone.

Then, in eighteen twenty-eight, a Dutchman invented a chocolate press, a machine which made it possible to produce solid chocolate as well as cocoa powder. This had a huge impact on the way chocolate was consumed, as people began to eat chocolate as well as just drinking it.

The significance of his invention was quickly understood and the first ever bars of chocolate were manufactured in a factory in England in eighteen forty-seven. Solid chocolate rapidly gained in popularity and boxes of chocolates became a favourite form of gift on birthdays, for example.

People had already begun to experiment by adding different things to chocolate such as sugar, eggs and spices but with the addition of milk, a Swiss man, Daniel Peter, was able to produce, in eighteen seventy-five, chocolate which was similar to what we would recognise as chocolate today.

The good news for chocolate eaters today is that it's not only delicious but it can also be good for you. Scientific studies have proved that chocolate has a positive effect on your mood. Some researchers also think that eating a little bit of dark chocolate every day can lower your blood pressure, but the results aren't conclusive.

So what I'd like to do now is move on to talk about how chocolate is made today and the most interesting thing …

[pause]

Now you'll hear Part Two again.

tone

[The recording is repeated.]

[pause]

That is the end of Part Two.

Now turn to Part Three.

[pause]

PART 3

You'll hear five short extracts in which teenagers are talking about a family day out at an activity centre. For questions 19–23, choose from the list (A–H) what each speaker says about the place they went to. Use the letters only once. There are three extra letters which you do not need to use.

You now have thirty seconds to look at Part Three.

[pause]

tone

Speaker 1

[pause]

Me and my brother have just spent a day at a dry ski slope with our dad. He's really good so sadly he went off on his own after he'd fixed us up with hired boots and skis. Then, we had our first lesson. In a group of six, we learnt all about walking, sliding, controlling speed and safety. It was a bit tough but we'd both like to keep going till we can do it properly. In fact, Mum's promised to get us our own boots and skis if we stick with it – we can go and have a holiday where there's proper snow. That'd be so brilliant.

[pause]

Speaker 2

[pause]

My mum found out about this climbing centre by chance and thought it'd be a fun thing for me to try with a friend. Before you go on the climbing wall, you have to learn some basic techniques and study the safety rules. As long as you're over twelve, though, you can go unaccompanied by a grown-up, which suited me fine actually. There was a shop selling all sorts of climbing gear and equipment for other sports too so my folks had somewhere to hang out. I hope to go again one day 'cause I'm keen to learn all sorts of climbing techniques.

[pause]

Speaker 3

[pause]

My parents took me and two friends to a fantastic outdoor activity park last weekend. It was a huge place with lots of amazing things to do. Like, quad bikes you could hire, boats you could row, a sort of rope path you could walk on through the treetops, an area for observing birds. We only saw and did about half of the things there, which was a bit disappointing so I hope we can go back soon. Mum and Dad did some of the activities with us – like we all went out in a boat together, but mostly they just sat and drank coffee while we did stuff.

[pause]

Speaker 4

[pause]

Last Saturday I got taken to a pottery studio. First we chose a plain piece of pottery – like a vase or bowl or whatever – and you had to decorate it – you could like paint it any way you liked. I did a mug and painted a heavy metal slogan on it. There were like staff around who could come to the rescue if you really messed up, but I managed on my own. When we'd finished, the stuff had to go in a sort of oven and we're going back next weekend to pick it up. I can't wait to see how it's turned out!

[pause]

Speaker 5

[pause]

Last weekend, my parents took me and two friends to this activity centre based around a strange underground cave. We went down really steep, long winding passages – the walls all decorated with shells, made into pretty patterns like mosaics. Dad told us that the place had been discovered by accident around a hundred and seventy years ago when a local farmer was digging out a pond, but that it's probably over five hundred years old. Nobody really knows who made it or what it was used for. I'd love to solve the mystery myself one day. Mum bought us some postcards in the souvenir shop, but we didn't bother going round the other stuff there.

[pause]

Now you'll hear Part Three again.

tone

[The recording is repeated.]

[pause]

That is the end of Part Three.

Now turn to Part Four.

[pause]

PART 4

You'll hear an interview with a girl called Poppy Wallace, who sings in a girl band called GirlSong. For questions 24–30, choose the best answer (A, B or C).

You now have one minute to look at Part Four.

[pause]

tone

Interviewer: Today I'm talking to Poppy Wallace, lead singer with GirlSong, the popular girl band. Poppy, GirlSong has been one of this year's most dramatic success stories. It must've been an exciting time for you.

Poppy: Absolutely. It's been amazing. We've been so lucky. We've had to do a lot of work over the past year, of course, and we only got together just before that. Everyone we met in the music business was always really excited about our sound and said we'd make it big, but none of us thought our time would come so soon. It's great that it has!

Interviewer: I'm sure. You've just completed your first international tour. How was that?

Poppy: It was great! We'd done a couple of short tours in this country so we were already reasonably confident in front of large audiences. But it was exciting to make new fans all over the world. It was just a pity we were moving on all the time and couldn't really get to know people. Next time, we'll try to build in more opportunities for contact with our fan base. As a band, we've got even closer to each other than we were before – which is brilliant! I know that sometimes things can become quite tense within groups on tour. I'm glad that didn't happen to us.

Interviewer: You were joined on tour by Leo, a singer who's been around for over ten years now. How did that come about?

Poppy: Well, we were doing some recording at the studios near here and at the end of the first day our agent told us he'd just seen Leo walking down the stairs. We joked about how good it would be to work together, never dreaming it'd actually happen. Next day, there was a message for us. The studio manager had asked Leo to listen to one of the tracks we'd recorded. He loved it and wanted to try doing something together. It really was a dream come true!

Interviewer: And you're going to be working with Leo again. Are you looking forward to it?

Poppy: Well, of course it'll be a great opportunity to record an album with him. I can't deny that. The thought of all those people pointing cameras at us everywhere we go, though, is quite scary really. I mean we're always having to write songs to deadlines and rehearse for long hours so we're used to that sort of stress.

Interviewer: When you're on an international tour, do you have time to enjoy yourselves?

Poppy: Up to a point. We play in some amazing places and I'd love to spend some time sightseeing – we rarely get the opportunity unfortunately. But I always find out how to say the basic things to people without using English and that's great fun. And before going anywhere, we try to find out a bit more about the folk music of the area and even watch other singers perform for a change.

Interviewer: Right. You come from Barbados. Do you often get back there?

Poppy: Well, though my family comes from Barbados, I was actually born in London – but I've always spent all of my holidays there because I've got lots of relatives on the island. The beaches are popular places for hanging out with friends. They're quite crowded though so sitting around strumming guitars with my mates in my uncle's garden – that's what does it for me! And then there's the food, that's pretty good too, of course.

Interviewer: As a young kid who was your special musical hero?

Poppy: I certainly had heroes but it was only when I got a bit older that I became a big fan of a local singer because I could really relate to her songs. When I was a kid, my idol was a girl from my favourite series of cartoon films. She had lots of adventures and I'm afraid I used to admire the way she'd ignore what her teacher told her to do in class. The only lessons I liked were geography and I did have a wonderful teacher – I appreciate that now – though I didn't realise it at the time.

Interviewer: Sure. And how about the …

[pause]

Now you'll hear Part Four again.

tone

[The recording is repeated.]

[pause]

That is the end of Part Four.

There will now be a pause of five minutes for you to copy your answers onto the separate answer sheet. Be sure to follow the numbering of all the questions. I'll remind you when there's one minute left so that you're sure to finish in time.

[Teacher, pause the recording here for five minutes. Remind students when they have one minute left.]

That is the end of the test. Please stop now. Your supervisor will now collect all the question papers and answer sheets.

Test 3 Key

Reading and Use of English (1 hour 15 minutes)

Part 1

1 D **2** B **3** C **4** A **5** B **6** D **7** C **8** A

Part 2

9 Not **10** to **11** across **12** it **13** unless **14** become / be
15 something **16** Give

Part 3

17 frightened **18** knowledge **19** impossible **20** daily / everyday
21 discovery **22** weaknesses **23** friendships **24** decisions

Part 4

25 WISH I'd / I had / I could have / I could've | seen
26 didn't / did not | TURN up
27 ALTHOUGH she / Lisa | did not / didn't feel OR
ALTHOUGH she / Lisa | was not / wasn't (feeling)
28 WHAT time | the bus leaves
29 is | INCLUDED in / with
30 was ALLOWED | to leave

Part 5

31 A **32** D **33** C **34** C **35** B **36** A

Part 6

37 E **38** C **39** B **40** G **41** D **42** F

Part 7

43 B **44** A **45** D **46** C **47** D **48** C **49** C
50 D **51** A **52** B

Writing (1 hour 20 minutes)

Candidate responses are marked using the assessment scale on page 108.

Listening (approximately 40 minutes)

Part 1

1 B **2** A **3** C **4** B **5** C **6** B **7** B **8** C

Part 2

9 lecturer / university lecturer / lecturer at (a/the) university
10 wave
11 radio
12 teeth
13 ear(s)
14 tail
15 submarine
16 50 / fifty
17 raincoat / rain(-)coat
18 eagles (flying)

Part 3

19 B **20** F **21** H **22** D **23** E

Part 4

24 C **25** A **26** B **27** B **28** B **29** A **30** C

Transcript

This is the Cambridge English: First for Schools, Test 3.

I'm going to give you the instructions for this test. I'll introduce each part of the test and give you time to look at the questions. At the start of each piece you'll hear this sound:

tone

You'll hear each piece twice.

Remember, while you're listening, write your answers on the question paper. You'll have five minutes at the end of the test to copy your answers onto the separate answer sheet.

There will now be a pause. Please ask any questions now, because you must not speak during the test.

[pause]

Now open your question paper and look at Part One.

[pause]

PART 1 *You'll hear people talking in eight different situations. For questions 1–8, choose the best answer (A, B or C).*

Question 1 *One. You hear a girl who is going to live in another country talking to a friend.*

[pause]

tone

Boy: Are you excited about your family moving to live in the USA for two years?

Girl: In a way. It sounds an interesting place. It'll be weird going to a new school and I'm going to miss my friends.

Boy: But you'll soon meet new ones and feel at home, I'm sure.

Girl: I know that, but we must keep in touch.

Boy: Yes, at least we can do that on our laptops and even see each other as we chat.

Girl: True, but there's going to be a big time difference. I'll be getting up just as you go to bed, I think.

Boy: Oh, I hadn't thought of that. What a pain!

[pause]

tone

[The recording is repeated.]

[pause]

Question 2 *Two. You hear part of a science programme about a planned space mission to the moons of Jupiter.*

[pause]

tone

Did you know many planets have their own moons? Well, plans are being made for a space mission to explore four moons of the planet Jupiter. It's hoped that it will launch in twenty twenty-two and the journey there will take eight years. Some interesting features make these moons well worth visiting. Three of the moons are thought to have oceans underneath their surfaces so it's possible there could be some form of life there. One, known as Ganymede, is the only moon in the solar system to have its own magnetic field. Another, called Io, is the most volcanically active body known to us, shooting material an amazing three hundred kilometres above its surface.

[pause]

tone

[The recording is repeated.]

[pause]

Question 3 *Three. You hear a girl telling her father about a writer who visited her school.*

[pause]

tone

Man: How was school today, Gemma?

Gemma: Great, thanks. A writer came to talk to us about his work.

Man: Oh. What was his name?

Gemma: I can't remember actually, Peter somebody ... But I knew he'd written over a hundred books and I actually want to read some of them now. He said he lives on an island in the middle of nowhere and that's where he gets all his ideas. There are some ancient ruins there and sometimes when he's wandering alone, he really feels the past coming to life. Anyway, he was there at the end signing his books so I was hoping to say hello. The queue was too long though. That was a pity.

[pause]

tone

[The recording is repeated.]

[pause]

Question 4 *Four. You hear part of an interview with a girl who is talking about some wolves she saw.*

[pause]

tone

Interviewer: Emma, I hear something exciting happened to you.

Emma: Yes, I live near a village in the mountains and last week I saw some wolves near my home. To get to school, it's a fifteen-minute walk through a small wood and I saw this wolf crossing my path about fifty metres away. It stopped and looked directly at me. I wasn't actually all that frightened. I took a photo with my phone just as it was walking away. Then, another day, I saw a much bigger one. I was glad it was on the other side of the river. I didn't have my phone with me then so that was a bit disappointing, but it was amazing to see another one in the same area.

[pause]

tone

[The recording is repeated.]

[pause]

Question 5 *Five. You hear a young racing driver talking on the radio.*

[pause]

tone

Man: I first got into motor sports when I was ten years old. I started karting and loved it but it's taken me years of hard work to get where I am now. It's really exciting to be racing in the World Series. I've already had one podium place, coming second in the first race of the new drivers' championship. You have to be fit to be a racing driver. The G-force that goes through your body is immense. We train three hours a day six days a week. To be among the winners in a race is a fantastic feeling. The only thing I dislike about racing is not winning.

[pause]

tone

[The recording is repeated.]

[pause]

Question 6 *Six. You overhear a boy talking about a football competition he has been in.*

[pause]

tone

Boy: After winning three rounds of the football competition, our team made it to the finals. Although we were quite nervous, we handled the pressure well. We got a lot of support from our teachers, chased every ball down, and we were worn out by the end. We were at a bit of a disadvantage though, as we were some of the youngest ones there, but that didn't put us off! Some people in the team thought we could have done better but we gave it our best effort. We eventually came ninth but even though we didn't come near to winning, we were proud to represent our school.

[pause]

tone

[The recording is repeated.]

[pause]

Question 7 *Seven. You overhear a girl talking about a club she has recently started going to.*

[pause]

tone

Girl: The club runs for two and a half hours on a Saturday morning. I've been going for a couple of months now and I get plenty of help. We create dishes from scratch and prepare everything from cakes and puddings to two-course meals. I can't do all that yet, of course! But the chef running it makes sure that we're all involved with the whole process from the initial preparation of ingredients right through to clearing away afterwards. That's something I'm not really too keen on! There are also speakers who come to talk to us about things like the importance of eating a healthy, well-balanced diet. So on the whole, it's good!

[pause]

tone

[The recording is repeated.]

[pause]

Question 8 *Eight. You hear a teacher talking to her class about some homework they did.*

[pause]

tone

Woman: I've marked your geography assignments and will give them back to you in a moment. I wanted to just make some general points about them first. On the whole, they were much better than the last pieces of work you did. You've really taken on board the points I made about labelling maps and tables. Most of you also used headings and sub-headings in an effective and appropriate way. Where you do need to improve now is in ensuring you avoid careless spelling and grammar errors. There were too many of these. If you'd just read your work through before printing it off, you'd have picked most of them up.

[pause]

tone

[The recording is repeated.]

[pause]

That is the end of Part One.

Now turn to Part Two.

[pause]

PART 2 *You'll hear a student called Emily giving a class presentation about a whale watching trip she went on with her family. For questions 9–18, complete the sentences with a word or short phrase.*

You now have forty-five seconds to look at Part Two.

[pause]

tone

Emily: Hello everyone. I want to tell you about an exciting time I had during the school holidays. I went on a whale watching trip with my family. We spent two days on a small boat with a local guide, who was called Luka. The boat we went on belonged to Luka's father who's a fisherman. Luka himself is a lecturer at the local university for nine months of the year and a guide only during the summer months. He was an excellent guide because he knew exactly where to find the whales. I needed him to point them out to me because when we started seeing them I had real trouble distinguishing a whale from a wave. That takes practice, believe me. Like my dad thought he saw one and it was just a bit of wood floating in the water!

There were about ten boats in the harbour near where we were staying and they took tourists on whale watching trips. They were all licensed by the local government and the guides all helped each other. So, for example, when one of them found a group of whales out at sea, they'd get on the radio to tell the others their position. A mobile phone just doesn't work offshore and there's no computer on board.

Over the two days, Luka gave us so much information that it's difficult to remember it all. For instance, I knew that some whales have a kind of voice and sometimes 'sing' but I was amazed to learn that many whales don't have teeth. And I also found out that there are actually over seventy different species of whale. I thought there were only about six.

One unusual fact that I don't think you'll have heard before about whales is that scientists can tell their age quite easily. I thought this would be from their size or from the markings on their skin, whereas actually scientists study the wax in their ears because this has layers that can be counted. I suppose it's a bit like counting the circles in a tree trunk to find out how long the tree's been standing.

When I saw my first whale, I noticed its tail was white and patchy, unlike its back, which was a normal dark blue colour. Luka said that lots of different tiny creatures live on the whale and they can make parts of it look white. These creatures include barnacles and sea lice. When I saw one large whale, its shape and the colour of its body reminded me less of a big fish like a shark, for example, and more of a submarine. It was brilliant!

Luka tried hard to get as close as possible to the whales and most of the time we were about seventy-five metres away from them. We weren't able to go closer than fifty because of regulations that are there for their protection. Anyway, the idea was for our boat to move quickly up behind the whale as it took in oxygen on the surface of the water before diving a hundred metres or so down to the sea bed again. On average, you have about eight to twelve minutes to take your photos before the whale makes its next dive.

If you get a chance to go whale watching, you should because it's a fantastic thing to do. My dad took a pair of binoculars with him and my mum had a camera, but what I think you really need is a raincoat. This is because when a whale breathes out, it sprays water everywhere and you can get completely soaked! When we were on the boat, we were hoping to see some dolphins as well because Luka said that sometimes people do manage to spot them. We were unlucky on the two days we went, but we did get to see some eagles flying close to land. That made up for it!

So that was what I did in my school holidays. Does anyone have any questions?

[pause]

Now you'll hear Part Two again.

tone

[The recording is repeated.]

[pause]

That is the end of Part Two.

Now turn to Part Three.

[pause]

PART 3

You'll hear five short extracts in which teenagers are talking about a new video game. For questions 19–23, choose from the list (A–H) the opinion each speaker expresses. Use the letters only once. There are three extra letters which you do not need to use.

You now have thirty seconds to look at Part Three.

[pause]

tone

Speaker 1

[pause]

Usually I play video games based on some kind of sport – the ones based on football or motor racing or skateboarding – that sort of thing. Once me and my friends start playing that kind of game we could keep playing all day. But I've just got a new game I love and it's rather different. It's a kind of adventure game where you have to solve different puzzles and work your way through a range of levels. It's hard to explain without showing it to you, but it's quite simple to play really. And the graphics are amazing. They got me into it actually because I don't usually go for this sort of game.

[pause]

Speaker 2

[pause]

My older brother gave me this game for my birthday. I think he really wanted it for himself 'cause he used to have the earlier version of the same game and loved it. So I guess it's really meant for people a bit older than me – but I'm slowly beginning to enjoy it. You have to pretend you're in charge of a city and make all sorts of decisions about what to do to make it all work efficiently. There's lots of different levels, but I haven't progressed past the second one yet! My brother keeps borrowing it and, needless to say, he's already on level six!

[pause]

Speaker 3

[pause]

A new version of Pets on Bikes has just come out and it's brilliant, just as great as the earlier versions. The graphics are new. They're more sophisticated and they're going to take a bit of getting used to, but it's introduced a lot of new levels. Before you start playing you can choose which pet you want to be. I play it with a mate of mine. We just stick with the choice we made when we first played it. I've never yet managed to beat him but I'm determined not to stop playing until I have. No matter how long it takes!

[pause]

Speaker 4

[pause]

My parents are always complaining about how much time I spend playing video games. They just can't understand why me and my best friend get so caught up with them. Anyway, I thought this new game might help them see the point 'cause it really is something that people of different ages can get into. You pick a car, then set off on a drive round the world, deciding your route and which mysteries you want to solve along the way. They loved it and spent ages discussing which car to go for and where to head first. I'm just hoping they'll stop all the nagging now.

[pause]

Speaker 5

[pause]

My friend's just lent me the latest version of our favourite football game. It's fun and very exciting to play. But then so are earlier versions. This one's got some interesting new features – once you work out how to operate them – though that's not as straightforward as it should be, in my opinion. The graphics are certainly impressive, but the visual element's not the main thing for me. Anyway, I don't think I'll bother buying this version myself, I'll just keep on playing the older game, which I don't think I'll ever get tired of. Especially since I usually manage to beat my friend when we play it!

[pause]

Now you'll hear Part Three again.

tone

[The recording is repeated.]

[pause]

That is the end of Part Three.

Now turn to Part Four.

[pause]

PART 4

You'll hear an interview with Jack Herbert, a talented young pianist. For questions 24–30, choose the best answer (A, B or C).

You now have one minute to look at Part Four.

[pause]

tone

Interviewer: Hi there. On today's programme, I'm talking to teenage concert pianist, Jack Herbert. Jack, tell us when and how you first started playing.

Jack: Well, my Gran played quite well – when I was a little kid, I'd drop off to sleep at night to the sound of her playing in the distance. It wasn't long before I was asking to have a go myself. Gran didn't fancy the idea of teaching me so she arranged for me to have lessons with a proper teacher. And wow – was he strict! But she was always there for me – making sure I kept going whenever things got tough and, you know, she'd find me interesting things to play, stuff like that.

Interviewer: Do you come from a very musical family?

Jack: My older sister's just graduated from music college and she's desperate to find a permanent position in an orchestra. She plays for a local theatre company from time to time, but it doesn't pay the bills so she's taken a job in a music store till she gets sorted out. And my brother's quite a talented guitarist who used to do gigs with a band but he's given it all up. Mum played in a national symphony orchestra before she married Dad. They've always been a great support to me. So I've been lucky really.

Interviewer: Now, at the age of twelve, you got a scholarship to the National Music School. What was it like there?

Jack: Well, obviously it was a huge privilege to play with the greatest young musicians in the country, though I didn't really appreciate it at the time. The thing was I didn't feel at home among all those talented people. I thought I'd never be good enough for my teachers there, though I really wanted to do my best. I had to do what were called 'performance platforms' – I'd play on a small stage in the hallway of the college. And the music they'd given me to play always seemed much too challenging. But I can see now that I needed to be pushed so I'm grateful to them.

Interviewer: Practising must take up a lot of your time.

Jack: It does – practice will always be part of my life, even if there's other stuff I'd rather be doing sometimes because you can't get to the top without putting the hours in. But of course, there's more to being a good concert pianist than just hours of endless practice.

Interviewer: What's important for you when you're actually performing?

Jack: Well, at school they encourage you to put your stamp on a performance, you know, make it into something personal. But when I'm actually on stage, I forget about all that. And I don't try for perfection either. I just try to get the audience to appreciate the music as much as I do. For me, that's what it's all about.

Interviewer: And what makes you different from other young pianists?

Jack: I'm not sure. There's loads of very talented young pianists out there and what's exciting is that because we're young, other teenagers are starting to take an interest in what we do. We're definitely seeing more of them coming to concerts. Some young musicians get popular by sort of jazzing up traditional pieces, giving them a modern trendy feel, which I don't actually do. And many of them stick to classical stuff whereas I'm prepared to branch out – there's no type of music I'm not willing to try.

Interviewer: So Jack, what are your plans for the future?

Jack: Well, for the time being, I'm happy doing what I'm doing. I'm headed for Germany later this month, though, 'cause I'm taking part in an international competition there. I need to go in for more of these if I want to get better known. My teachers have encouraged me to try writing pieces of my own, and I've done a bit of that, but it's pretty obvious that's not where my strengths lie.

Interviewer: Well, Jack – thanks very much for talking to us today.

[pause]

Now you'll hear Part Four again.

tone

[The recording is repeated.]

[pause]

That is the end of Part Four.

There will now be a pause of five minutes for you to copy your answers onto the separate answer sheet. Be sure to follow the numbering of all the questions. I'll remind you when there's one minute left so that you're sure to finish in time.

[Teacher, pause the recording here for five minutes. Remind students when they have one minute left.]

That is the end of the test. Please stop now. Your supervisor will now collect all the question papers and answer sheets.

Test 4 Key

Reading and Use of English (1 hour 15 minutes)

Part 1

1 A **2** B **3** D **4** A **5** B **6** C **7** D **8** C

Part 2

9 would / could / might / can **10** needs / has **11** order **12** out / on **13** like
14 but / except **15** the / what **16** how

Part 3

17 Mexican **18** evidence **19** exciting **20** remarkable **21** significance
22 disagreement **23** discoveries **24** generally

Part 4

25 in CASE | it gets / becomes / turns / is
26 WISH I hadn't / had not | eaten
27 for | NOT doing / completing / finishing OR for | NOT having done / completed / finished
28 I would / I'd | have CAUGHT OR I would've | CAUGHT
29 it | wasn't / was not UNTIL
30 MUST have | gone

Part 5

31 C **32** C **33** A **34** B **35** D **36** B

Part 6

37 D **38** F **39** A **40** G **41** E **42** C

Part 7

43 C **44** D **45** B **46** C **47** A **48** D **49** B **50** A
51 B **52** D

Writing (1 hour 20 minutes)

Candidate responses are marked using the assessment scale on page 108.

Listening (approximately 40 minutes)

Part 1

1 A **2** A **3** A **4** B **5** A **6** A **7** C **8** C

Part 2

9 zoo **10** farmers **11** repairs **12** night work **13** wild dog / Wild Dog
14 (animal) reserves **15** the Internet OR Internet use **16** lake **17** (heavy) boots
18 gloves

Part 3

19 C **20** G **21** A **22** B **23** F

Part 4

24 A **25** B **26** B **27** C **28** A **29** B **30** A

Transcript

This is the Cambridge English: First for Schools, Test 4.

I'm going to give you the instructions for this test. I'll introduce each part of the test and give you time to look at the questions. At the start of each piece you'll hear this sound:

tone

You'll hear each piece twice.

Remember, while you're listening, write your answers on the question paper. You'll have five minutes at the end of the test to copy your answers onto the separate answer sheet.

There will now be a pause. Please ask any questions now, because you must not speak during the test.

[pause]

Now open your question paper and look at Part One.

[pause]

PART 1

You'll hear people talking in eight different situations. For questions 1–8, choose the best answer (A, B or C).

Question 1

One. You overhear two friends talking about a lesson they had at school.

[pause]

tone

Girl: That was a brilliant science lesson, wasn't it?

Boy: Yes, but I find it hard to get my head round some of those facts that astronomers have recently discovered. You know, like they think that it's fifty thousand degrees Celsius on that star they're researching. How can that be?

Girl: I know what you mean. Or like it's a hundred and fifty times bigger than our sun. No wonder scientists are keen to find out more about it.

Boy: That's right. They want to discover why it's on its own rather than in a cluster of other stars, like they usually are. It's very curious, isn't it?

Girl: Sure is. I'd love to know the answer.

[pause]

tone

[The recording is repeated.]

[pause]

Question 2 *Two. You hear two friends talking about buying a card game for the boy's sister.*

[pause]

tone

Boy: Shall I get this card game for my sister's birthday?

Girl: How old is she? Seven?

Boy: That's right. Do you think it's too old for her?

Girl: Well, I didn't get it till I was ten, but I played it with my younger brother and he sometimes managed to beat me. It's quite easy once you get the hang of it, though it's hard at first to remember all the rules.

Boy: So you need a bit of patience? My sister hasn't got any!

Girl: That could be a problem then. Look, this board game here might be better.

Boy: Thanks. That's certainly the sort of thing she'd enjoy.

[pause]

tone

[The recording is repeated.]

[pause]

Question 3 *Three. You hear part of an interview on the radio with a writer of children's books.*

[pause]

tone

Interviewer: Do you think films and TV have made storybooks less important for children today?

Writer: I don't think anything will ever replace books. They're the most intimate form of entertainment 'cause they make strange worlds and characters come alive for you. You can experience everything in your own way – thrills, fear, sadness – and you feel as if you're part of the story yourself. Films are, somehow, much more of a shared experience. You see and feel exactly what everyone else sees and feels. I'm not saying films aren't powerful too. A good film will stay with you forever just as a good book will.

[pause]

tone

[The recording is repeated.]

[pause]

Question 4 *Four. You hear a guide speaking to tourists.*

[pause]

tone

Guide: There are many fascinating things to see and people to talk to here at Barrow Hill Living Museum. The museum covers a large site and you'll find different exhibits open on different days and at different times of year. But whenever you choose to visit, you're sure to see an excellent range of exhibits and demonstrations, some indoors, others outside. It's up to you which order you see them in and how long you spend in each area. Some exhibits are simple displays for you to enjoy, others are staffed by actors who'll help to bring the past to life and answer any questions you may have.

[pause]

tone

[The recording is repeated.]

[pause]

Question 5 *Five. You hear two friends talking about a music festival they are going to attend.*

[pause]

tone

Man: I think it should be a great festival this year, don't you? Even better than last year's.

Woman: You're right! There are gonna be the same brilliant people there. There's that group, South Redemption. They were just amazing last year.

Man: Yes, I didn't see them but I like their songs. And as well as all the people they've already announced, they're promising an appearance by someone really famous.

Woman: I wonder who that could be.

Man: Well, they've said someone fantastic's going to be performing with Fatima Wheatley, someone she's never worked with before. I can't wait to find out who that'll be. And Fatima's got a great voice, of course – I did get to see her perform last year.

Woman: Yes, me too.

[pause]

tone

[The recording is repeated.]

[pause]

Question 6 *Six. You hear two friends talking about a movie.*

[pause]

tone

Man: Did you enjoy the movie, Melissa?

Woman: I actually liked it even more than the book it was based on – which I loved. The actors were brilliant – perfect for their roles.

Man: Well, some were. I've read the book too and I thought the hero should've been someone a bit taller and darker. But the others were OK. And at least the director didn't mess around with the story.

Woman: No, thank goodness. It would've spoilt things if he had. I was a bit disappointed by some of the visual effects – especially in the car chase – but otherwise it was great.

Man: Oh? I was actually quite impressed by that chase!

[pause]

tone

[The recording is repeated.]

[pause]

Question 7 *Seven. You hear two friends talking about a news story about a baby monkey.*

[pause]

tone

Man: Did you see that news item about that really unusual monkey?

Woman: You mean the baby one born in the French zoo? It was the cutest thing I've ever seen! I wish I was the zookeeper looking after it!

Man: I don't know about that. But it's such a pity that there's only a thousand of them left in the world.

Woman: It is a shame, but at least this one's getting well cared for.

Man: Yes, but it would be better off in the wild where it belongs.

Woman: I'm not so sure. It's safe and it's got plenty to eat where it is!

Man: It's not the same, though, as having a forest to roam around in, is it?

[pause]

tone

[The recording is repeated.]

[pause]

Question 8 *Eight. You overhear two friends talking about their holidays.*

[pause]

tone

Girl: How was your holiday, Ben? You went to New York, didn't you?

Boy: Actually, my dad decided against that in the end. We went to the mountains instead. My parents said they wanted some fresh air and a more active holiday.

Girl: Well, that sounds good too.

Boy: Mm. I was quite disappointed at first but I came round to it a bit when they said I could have some skiing lessons if I wanted. And now I'm so glad we went. I can't wait to go again.

Girl: Oh, I didn't know you could ski.

Boy: I couldn't. But I can now. My instructor was great.

[pause]

tone

[The recording is repeated.]

[pause]

That is the end of Part One.

Now turn to Part Two.

[pause]

PART 2

You'll hear a student called Shirley Bailey giving a talk at her school about her experience of working at a wildlife centre in Africa last summer. For questions 9–18, complete the sentences with a word or short phrase.

You now have forty-five seconds to look at Part Two.

[pause]

tone

Shirley: Hi, everyone. Most of you know my name's Shirley. What you may not know is that I'm completely mad about animals and I wanted to work with them last summer. I've helped out at a horse riding school quite a bit, so I fancied something more exotic and I thought about the zoo. Fortunately, there's one close to where my Gran lives. When I enquired though, they'd already taken on their holiday staff, so I searched the Internet and found a wildlife centre called Greenwood in Namibia, which for those of you who aren't great at geography, like me, is in southern Africa. I applied and spent six fantastic weeks there.

Greenwood don't only look after animals – they also train volunteer students like me and talk to the farmers about the benefits of conservation and the fact that tourists now are so keen to pay to see wildlife. So protecting the animals can actually bring in money, which is very much needed when the crops don't do well.

The main job of a volunteer is, of course, to care for the animals, but I did do other things too, like doing repairs round the place, which was the most difficult thing because of the heat. I also did more laid-back tasks, like showing visitors round and answering loads of questions.

My daily routine included feeding the animals, which was great fun, and cleaning out their enclosures – a horribly dirty job, as you'd expect. We also had a schedule for night work with the babies. I thought I'd hate it as generally I need my sleep! Staying awake the next day was certainly tricky, but I was amazed that I actually looked forward to watching over the little ones and holding them if they woke up.

Over the past thirty years, Greenwood has been involved in the care of orphaned animals, including wild cats such as lions, leopards and cheetahs. But I was lucky enough to be working on what they referred to as the Wild Dog project, which involved identifying animals that need help, looking at family patterns of behaviour and recording their eating habits. I really loved it!

Greenwood has developed really great systems for getting animals back to health. The aim, then, is to move them on from the centre if they can. It would be wonderful to set them free into their natural habitat, though that hardly ever happens, as they've become too used to being helped by humans. So they are usually moved to animal reserves, where they can be checked up on from time to time.

Volunteers pay a weekly contribution to the centre in advance to cover accommodation and food, local transport and so on. You have to add flights on top, of course, but there really isn't much else to budget for once you're here except Internet use – as there aren't any shops selling souvenirs and that sort of thing nearby.

While you're at Greenwood, you stay in basic wooden cabins with three other volunteers. There's a sort of wooden balcony with armchairs, where we relaxed in the evening. What's great is that the cabins overlook a lake, so you can see different wild creatures coming to drink there in the evenings. It made a change after long days working at the centre.

So what about the stuff we had to take? I mainly packed shorts and T-shirts because it's very hot in the daytime. I thought initially that sandals would be useful, though we were told to bring heavy boots for protection when we were dealing with large animals.

The management also insisted that we wore gloves during our work time, which they always had a large supply of at the centre. That was very sensible, as was the instruction to bring a torch as the sun sets very quickly and it's so dark without street lights. Fortunately, I found a very powerful small one online and stuck that in my rucksack. It was so useful.

Now let me show you some pictures of the animals I liked best ...

[pause]

Now you'll hear Part Two again.

tone

[The recording is repeated.]

[pause]

That is the end of Part Two.

Now turn to Part Three.

[pause]

PART 3

You'll hear five short extracts in which teenagers are talking about the sports they take part in. For questions 19–23, choose from the list (A–H) what each speaker says about their sport. Use the letters only once. There are three extra letters which you do not need to use.

You now have thirty seconds to look at Part Three.

[pause]

tone

Speaker 1

[pause]

I've always loved all kinds of sport. Two years ago, I decided to join a local running club. That meant buying stuff like running shorts, of course, and proper running shoes, which are different from ordinary trainers. It's a good thing I enjoy running because I didn't realise quite what a commitment being in a club would be. A competition can last anything from an afternoon to a whole weekend – then there's several nights' training every week too. What's great now is that my brother and some of my friends have joined the club as well. We have such a great time that we don't even mind if the weather's not brilliant.

[pause]

Speaker 2

[pause]

I joined a hockey club near where we live. I love it, even though I'm usually pretty tired after a game 'cause it involves lots of running. You get really dirty too, but I don't mind that. My aunt got me into it and even lent me some kit, you know the stick, special boots and padding. The ball's quite hard so you need to be protected against injury. I'm quite glad I'm not in goal 'cause the keeper has to wear a helmet and even more padding. We practise for one or two hours each week, then play against other teams most weekends.

[pause]

Speaker 3

[pause]

When I was younger, I played tennis with my cousin. We went to a kids' summer course and had great fun, so I decided to take it up seriously and I joined a club. I really improved, but I was worried when my coach suggested I was ready to do competitions. I found I liked them more than I expected to, though. Then I twisted my ankle during training and I couldn't play for several weeks. I was upset about that, but I'm back to playing now and it's great because the club has recently built a couple of new courts for us to use.

[pause]

Speaker 4

[pause]

I've got a basketball hoop at home and I'm always practising and trying out new moves with my best friend. So it was great when our school decided to get a basketball team together. We were given our team shirts, but not trainers, and we all had to buy a mouthguard to protect our teeth as well. We practise about three hours every week and have to do running and keep-fit exercises too. Mum's booked me into the basketball camp for the school holidays next month. They've got great coaches and I should be able to make some progress with my ball-handling techniques for competitions against other schools next year.

[pause]

Speaker 5

[pause]

I love riding my bike. So when a cycling club for teenagers started in my area, I couldn't wait to sign up and Dad eventually agreed to pay for it. Now I race both on roads and on a special track. I really enjoy the training sessions as well as the competitions we sometimes do. And I don't mind how long I spend out on my bike, except when it's wet – that can make things a bit miserable. Some of my friends have joined the club too. Of course, you can get problems with your bike when you're racing, so we've all had to do a course in how to do bike repairs.

[pause]

Now you'll hear Part Three again.

tone

[The recording is repeated.]

[pause]

That is the end of Part Three.

Now turn to Part Four.

[pause]

PART 4

You'll hear part of an interview with Roberto Gianni. For questions 24–30, choose the best answer (A, B or C).

You now have one minute to look at Part Four.

[pause]

tone

Interviewer: Today in the studio we have twenty-five year-old Roberto Gianni, who's one of the country's youngest successful fashion designers. Roberto's going to answer questions sent in by teenage listeners. First up, Rachel, who's fifteen, asks: 'What made you want to design clothes?'

Roberto: I used to go to a youth club which had a fashion workshop. It was basically a lot of teenagers customising clothes. That is, they'd take fairly boring jeans or T-shirts and sew stuff on or cut bits out and stitch other bits on. I went with friends. We wanted to make our clothes stand out in a crowd, but I got a bit bored after a while 'cause I wanted to follow my own designs and do things from scratch. So I decided to make something to prove to my mates that I could do that.

Interviewer: So what happened then? Jamie, from Edinburgh, asks how you broke into the fashion industry.

Roberto: Well, the people at the youth club were quite impressed with what I'd made, but actually I was still at college and had no real interest in fashion at all at that stage. Anyway, the leaders at the youth club put me in for a competition. It was sponsored by a well-known fashion magazine. I ended up with first prize for the things I'd done and doors started opening pretty soon after that!

Interviewer: Next, Irina, who's sixteen, asks: 'How do you feel about your current designs?'

Roberto: My very first creation at the youth club was an evening dress for my sister. It took me some time 'cause I'd never sewn before. Amazingly, what I produced wasn't too bad. I then did some kids' clothes for my nephews and nieces. They seemed pleased with the result. So I branched out a bit and did some menswear, which came in for a lot of praise. But I knew I could do even better. These days I'm managing to create a modern urban look. It appeals to me anyway!

Interviewer: Next, Graham asks: 'What or who is your biggest influence when it comes to fashion?'

Roberto: That's a tricky one. I guess most people would say that it's someone really well-known – designers like Paul Smith or Alexander MacQueen. I'm nostalgic about the style of clothes in the 1950s that's reflected in my work. Of course, I go to all the big fashion shows, but I try to make sure that what I see there doesn't change what I'm doing too much.

Interviewer: Now, your sister's quite a famous model. Mike asks if all your family's in the fashion business.

Roberto: Not at all, no. When my parents found out I wanted to design clothes, they didn't know quite what to think. They'd assumed I'd go into education – they're both teachers – but they realised I was determined, so they backed me all the way. They knew once I'd made up my mind, that was it.

Interviewer: Paul, from London, wants to know how you cope with criticism.

Roberto: The public sometimes doesn't go for individuality and I try not to take any negative comments to heart – though that's tough sometimes. I just carry on regardless because I have a faith in what I do, and that's not easily shaken. There's always a feeling with some people that everyone has to look the same. That's not something I'm into, but I don't mind them being like that.

Interviewer: Finally, a number of people have asked if you have any advice for young people trying to get into the fashion industry today.

Roberto: I guess, know yourself. This industry can crush you, change your views and change you. This can happen, especially if you do a traditional college course, even a good one. I'd say, get a job where you're also going to get some training, like with a photographer or on a magazine. Put together a portfolio which shows a few of your ideas, don't go over the top on this though.

Interviewer: Roberto, many thanks for coming …

[pause]

Now you'll hear Part Four again.

tone

[The recording is repeated.]

[pause]

That is the end of Part Four.

There will now be a pause of five minutes for you to copy your answers onto the separate answer sheet. Be sure to follow the numbering of all the questions. I'll remind you when there's one minute left, so that you're sure to finish in time.

[Teacher, pause the recording here for five minutes. Remind students when they have one minute left.]

That is the end of the test. Please stop now. Your supervisor will now collect all the question papers and answer sheets.

CAMBRIDGE ENGLISH
Language Assessment
Part of the University of Cambridge

SAMPLE

Candidate Name
If not already printed, write name in CAPITALS and complete the Candidate No. grid (in pencil).

Candidate Signature

Examination Title

Centre

Supervisor:
If the candidate is ABSENT or has WITHDRAWN shade here

Centre No.

Candidate No.

Examination Details

0	0	0	0
1	1	1	1
2	2	2	2
3	3	3	3
4	4	4	4
5	5	5	5
6	6	6	6
7	7	7	7
8	8	8	8
9	9	9	9

Candidate Answer Sheet

Instructions

Use a PENCIL (B or HB).

Rub out any answer you wish to change using an eraser.

Parts 1, 5, 6 and 7:
Mark ONE letter for each question.

For example, if you think **B** is the right answer to the question, mark your answer sheet like this:

0	A	B	C	D

Parts 2, 3 and 4:
Write your answer clearly in CAPITAL LETTERS.

For Parts 2 and 3 write one letter in each box. For example:

0	E	X	A	M	P	L	E

Part 1

1	A	B	C	D
2	A	B	C	D
3	A	B	C	D
4	A	B	C	D
5	A	B	C	D
6	A	B	C	D
7	A	B	C	D
8	A	B	C	D

Part 2

		Do not write below here
9		9 1 0 u
10		10 1 0 u
11		11 1 0 u
12		12 1 0 u
13		13 1 0 u
14		14 1 0 u
15		15 1 0 u
16		16 1 0 u

Continues over →

Part 3

		Do not write below here
17		1 0 u
18		1 0 u
19		1 0 u
20		1 0 u
21		1 0 u
22		1 0 u
23		1 0 u
24		1 0 u

Part 4

		Do not write below here
25		2 1 0 u
26		2 1 0 u
27		2 1 0 u
28		2 1 0 u
29		2 1 0 u
30		2 1 0 u

Part 5

31	A B C D
32	A B C D
33	A B C D
34	A B C D
35	A B C D
36	A B C D

Part 6

37	A B C D E F G
38	A B C D E F G
39	A B C D E F G
40	A B C D E F G
41	A B C D E F G
42	A B C D E F G

Part 7

43	A B C D E F
44	A B C D E F
45	A B C D E F
46	A B C D E F
47	A B C D E F
48	A B C D E F
49	A B C D E F
50	A B C D E F
51	A B C D E F
52	A B C D E F

CAMBRIDGE ENGLISH
Language Assessment
Part of the University of Cambridge

SAMPLE

Candidate Name
If not already printed, write name in CAPITALS and complete the Candidate No. grid (in pencil).

Candidate Signature

Examination Title

Centre

Supervisor:
If the candidate is ABSENT or has WITHDRAWN shade here

Centre No.

Candidate No.

Examination Details

0	0	0	0
1	1	1	1
2	2	2	2
3	3	3	3
4	4	4	4
5	5	5	5
6	6	6	6
7	7	7	7
8	8	8	8
9	9	9	9

Candidate Answer Sheet

Instructions

Use a PENCIL (B or HB).
Rub out any answer you wish to change using an eraser.

Parts 1, 3 and 4:
Mark ONE letter for each question.

For example, if you think **B** is the right answer to the question, mark your answer sheet like this:

0 A B C

Part 2:
Write your answer clearly in CAPITAL LETTERS.

Write one letter or number in each box.
If the answer has more than one word, leave one box empty between words.

For example:

0 AN EXAMPLE

Turn this sheet over to start.

Part 1

1	A	B	C
2	A	B	C
3	A	B	C
4	A	B	C
5	A	B	C
6	A	B	C
7	A	B	C
8	A	B	C

Part 2 (Remember to write in CAPITAL LETTERS or numbers)

Do not write below here

9		9 1 0 u
10		10 1 0 u
11		11 1 0 u
12		12 1 0 u
13		13 1 0 u
14		14 1 0 u
15		15 1 0 u
16		16 1 0 u
17		17 1 0 u
18		18 1 0 u

Part 3

19	A	B	C	D	E	F	G	H
20	A	B	C	D	E	F	G	H
21	A	B	C	D	E	F	G	H
22	A	B	C	D	E	F	G	H
23	A	B	C	D	E	F	G	H

Part 4

24	A	B	C
25	A	B	C
26	A	B	C
27	A	B	C
28	A	B	C
29	A	B	C
30	A	B	C

Thanks and acknowledgements

The authors and publishers acknowledge the following sources of copyright material and are grateful for the permissions granted. While every effort has been made, it has not always been possible to identify the sources of all the material used, or to trace all copyright holders. If any omissions are brought to our notice, we will be happy to include the appropriate acknowledgements on reprinting.

Text acknowledgements

Straw Hat for the text on p. 14 adapted from *Queen Rider*. Copyright © Straw Hat Publishers 2014; The Toronto Star for the text on p. 16 adapted from 'Toronto Teens Send Lego Man on a Balloon Odyssey 24 Kilometers High' by Kate Allen, *The Toronto Star*, 25.01.2012. Copyright © 2012 by *The Toronto Star*; Redwings Horse Sanctuary for the text on p. 32 adapted from 'All About Horses…' www.redwings.org.uk. Copyright © The Redwings Horse Sanctuary; Random House Canada for the text on p. 36 adapted from *First Descent* by Pam Withers. Copyright © 2011 by Pam Withers; Dogo News for the text on p. 38 adapted from 'Need Electricity? Play a Game of Soccer!' by Meera Dolasia, 01.08.2012. Copyright © 2012 by Dogo News; text on p. 60 adapted from 'The History of Rollercoasters.' ThrillNetwork.com.

Photo acknowledgements

Key: T = Top, C = Centre, B = Below.

C1(T): Getty Images/© Ramiro Olaciregui; C1(B): Getty Images/© Ariel Skelley; C2(T): Getty Images/© Bob Thomas; C2(B): Corbis/© Andersen Ross/Blend Ross; C4(T): Getty Images/© Tyler Edwards/Digital Vision; C4(B): Getty Images/© Dennis Hallinan; C5(T): Corbis©/Kerrick James; C5(B): Getty Images/© Vicky Kasala/ Digital Vision; C7(T): Getty Images/© LWA; C7(B):Getty Images/ © Peter Dazeley; C8(T): Alamy/© Blend Images; C8(B): Corbis/© Maxie Productions/Blend Images; C10(T): Alamy/© Martyn Williams; C10(B): Alamy/© Alvey & Towers Picture Library; C11(T): Alamy/© David Willis; C11(B): Corbis/© Franz-Marc Frei; p.60 (Test 3, Part 6): Shutterstock/© Tom Hirtreifer.

The recordings which accompany this book were made at dsound, London.

Visual materials for the Speaking test

Why do you think the people have chosen to do these things on their family holiday?

1A

1B

Why do you think the people are celebrating in these situations?

1C

1D

1E

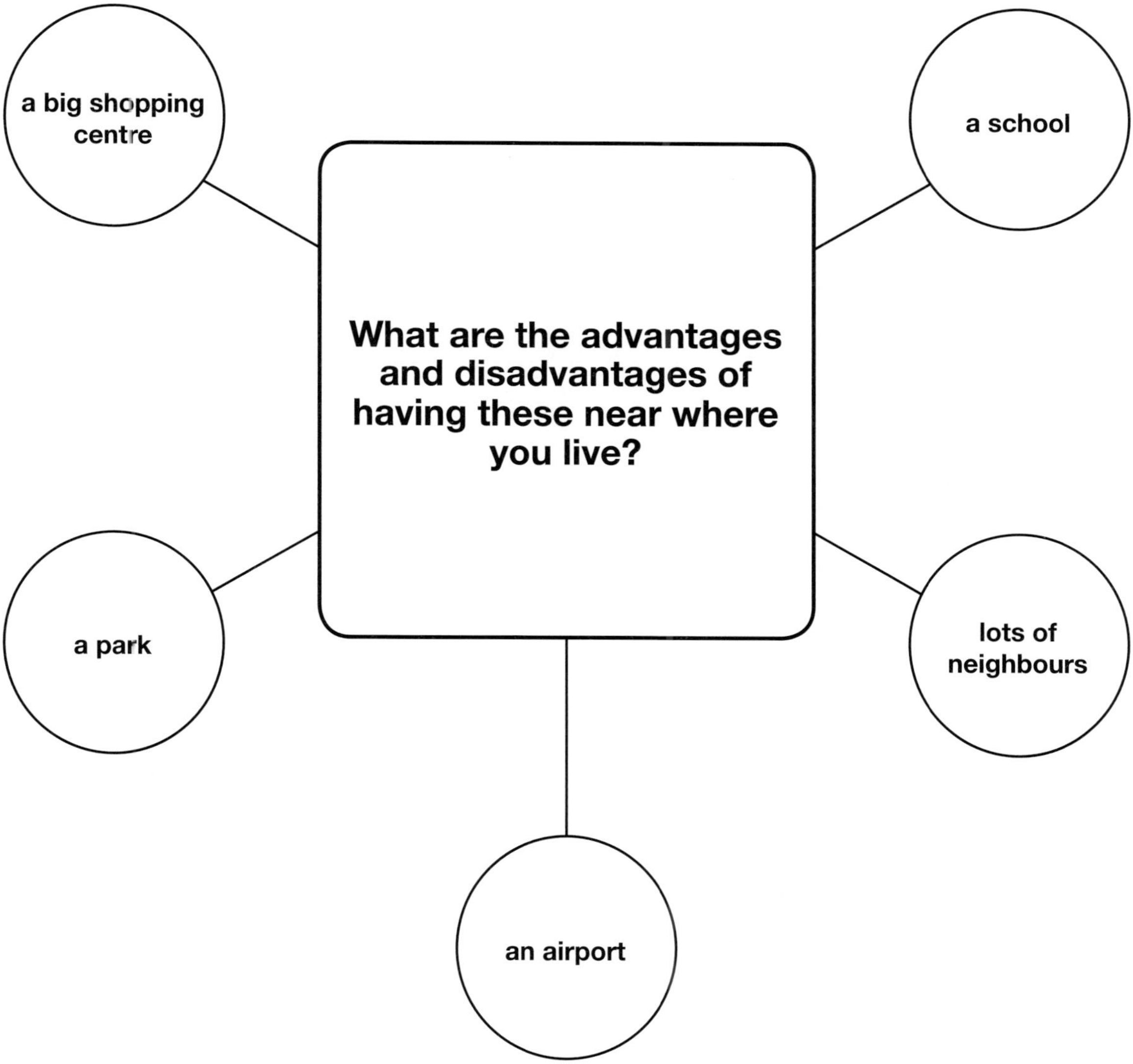
What are the advantages and disadvantages of having these near where you live?
a big shopping centre
a school
a park
lots of neighbours
an airport

Why do you think the people are cooking in these situations?

2A

2B

Why do you think the people are taking photographs in these situations?

2C

2D

2E

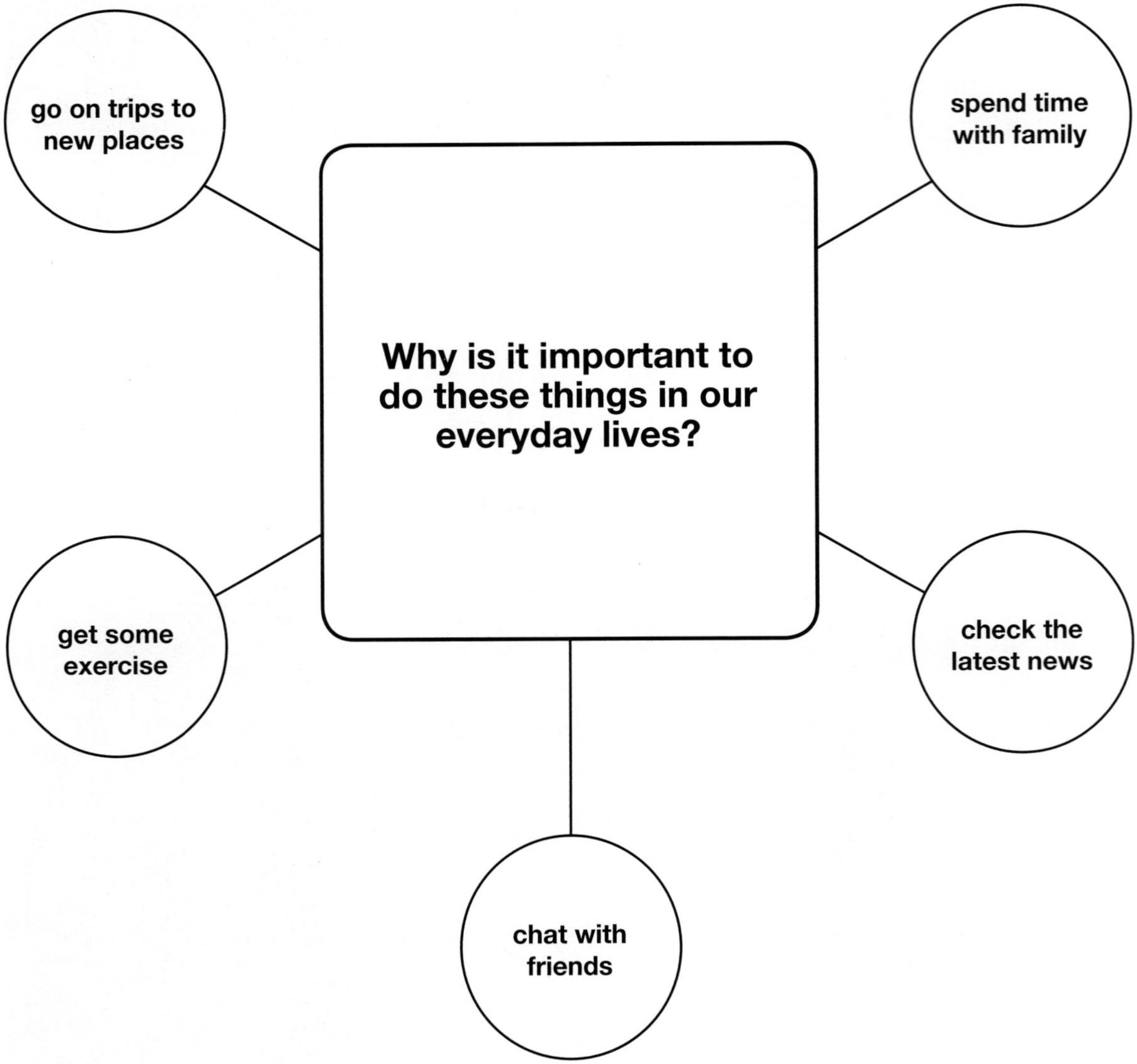
go on trips to new places
spend time with family
Why is it important to do these things in our everyday lives?
get some exercise
check the latest news
chat with friends

Why do you think the people need help in these situations?

3A

3B

Why do you think the people have chosen to do these things in town?

3C

3D

3E

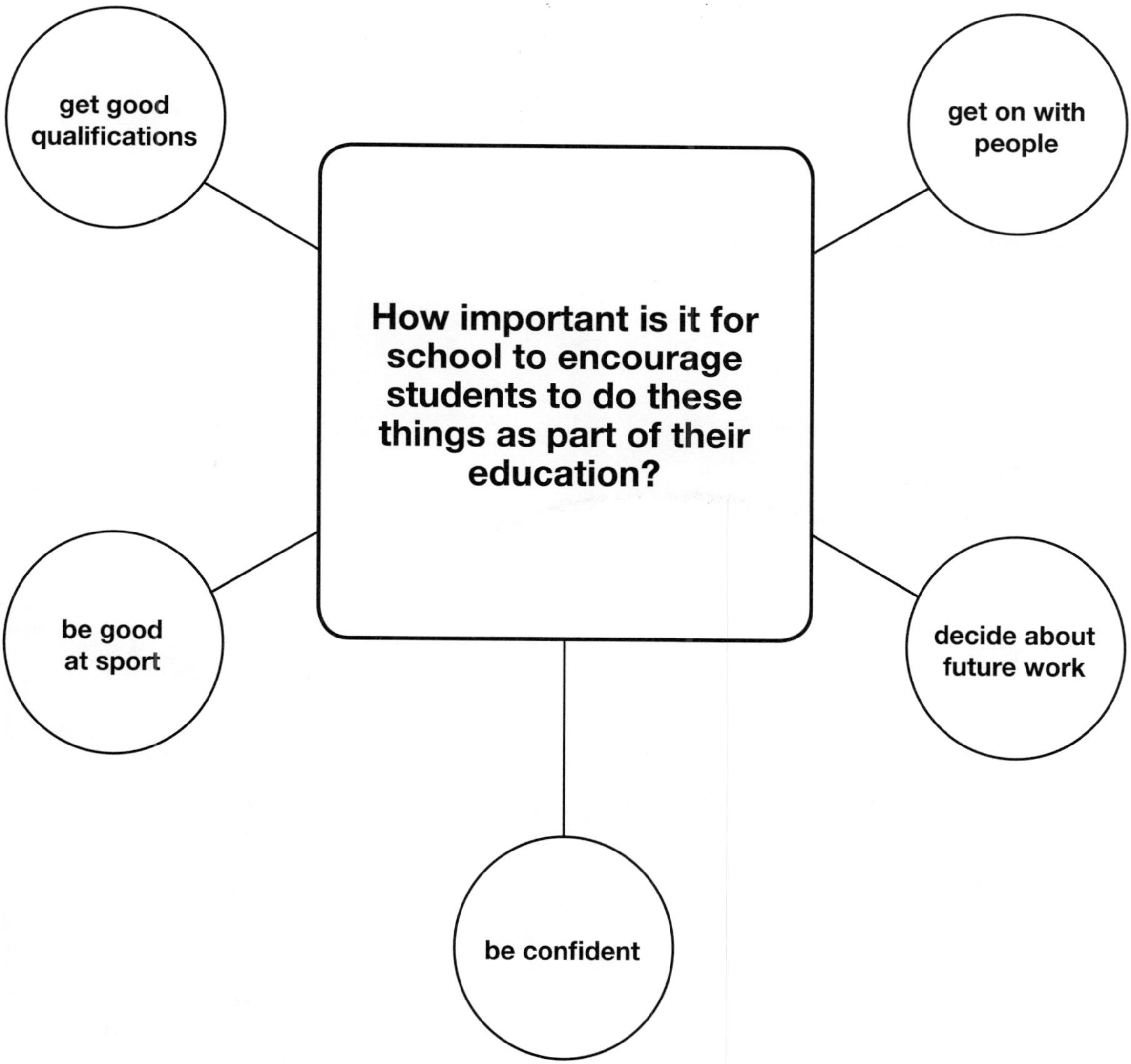
How important is it for school to encourage students to do these things as part of their education?
get good qualifications
get on with people
be good at sport
decide about future work
be confident

What do you think might be difficult for people travelling around a city in these ways?

4A

4B

Why do you think the people are enjoying doing these things on a free afternoon?

4C

4D

4E

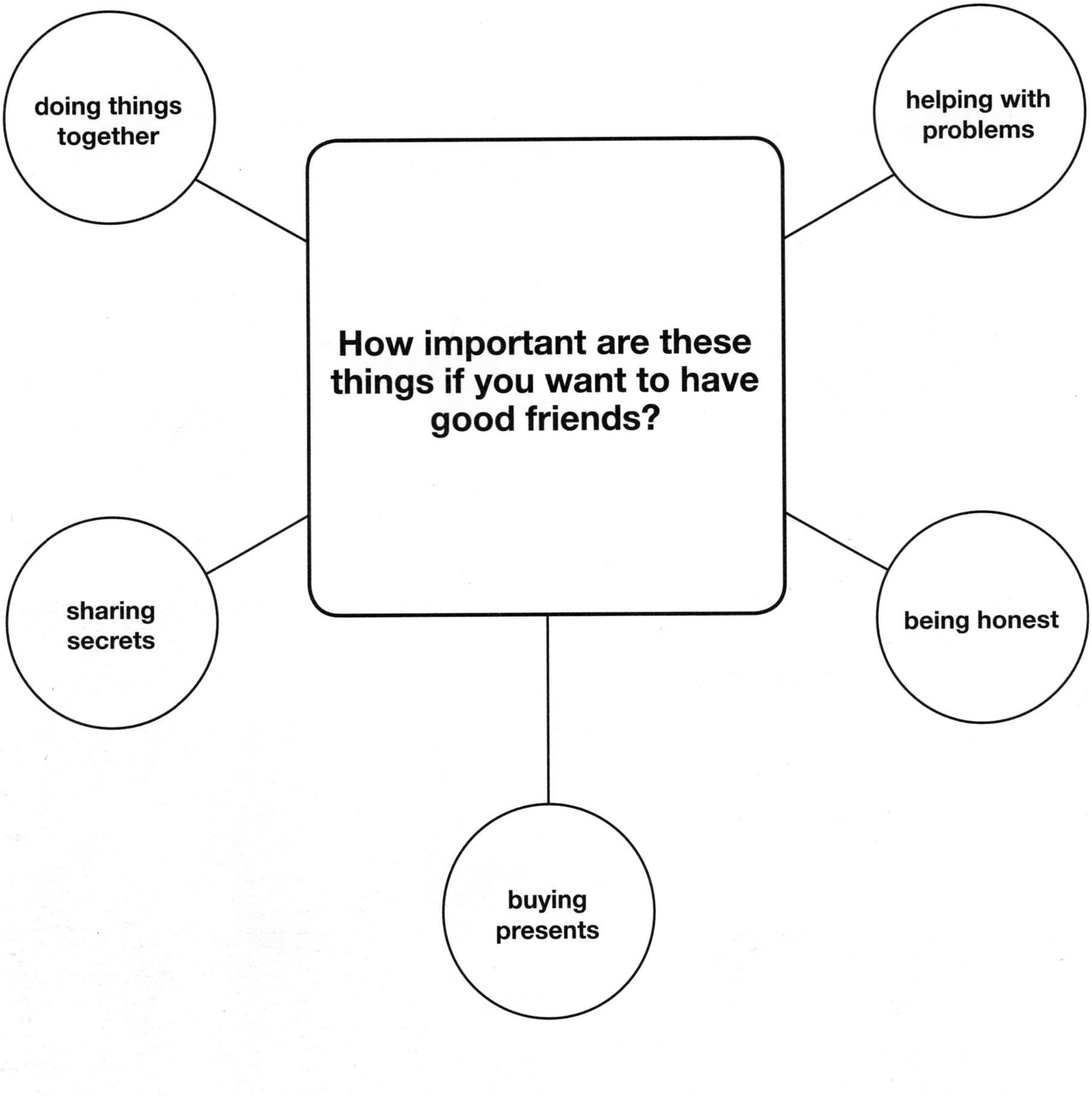
How important are these things if you want to have good friends?
doing things together
helping with problems
sharing secrets
being honest
buying presents